THE ROLE
of the
STATE LEGISLATURES
in the
CONFEDERACY

MAY SPENCER RINGOLD

THE ROLE
of the
STATE LEGISLATURES
in the
CONFEDERACY

UNIVERSITY OF GEORGIA PRESS • ATHENS

To

MY CHILDREN

COPYRIGHT © 1966

UNIVERSITY OF GEORGIA PRESS

LIBRARY OF CONGRESS CATALOG CARD NUMBER: 66-27607

PRINTED IN THE UNITED STATES BY FOOTE & DAVIES, DORAVILLE

CONTENTS

★

PREFACE

When Professor Charles W. Ramsdell inaugurated the Walter L. Fleming lectures in 1937 at Louisiana State University, his general topic was "Behind the Lines in the Southern Confederacy." Professor Ramsdell died before revising, expanding, and documenting the lectures, which remained in suggestive rather than definitive form. Their posthumous publication in 1944 afforded stimulating and provocative glimpses of the internal problems plaguing state and Confederate governments and inspired the research which has produced this book.

The Confederate Constitution, adopted on March 11, 1861, failed to incorporate concise statements of state rights. Yet the preamble emphasized the "sovereign and independent character" of the Confederate states; and the section which enumerated the powers of the Confederate Congress did not include "general welfare" among those purposes for which taxes could be levied and collected. By implication, then, general welfare became the constitutional province of the "sovereign and independent" states. The Confederate Congress, under pressure of conviction and necessity, left to the states a wide range of domestic activity.

This study of state legislatures in the Confederacy concentrates on the programs by which governors and general assemblies sought to relieve crises at home and to protect and maintain as nearly as possible normal economic, social, and political institutions. Secession conventions are a part of the investigation insofar as their ordinances initiated or supplemented policies of the legislatures.

In essence, the book deals with practical rather than

theoretical aspects of state rights in action. It is not concerned with abstract principles of government, nor does it seek to make a case for or against Confederate polity. It does point up difficulties common to the states of the Confederacy and examines the various attempts to surmount them. Moreover, it describes in the light of deteriorating local and national conditions the ultimate failure of the states to meet the physical needs and maintain the morale of the Southern people.

A substantial grant from the Southern Fellowships Fund and the assistance of Emory University in obtaining indispensable primary materials on microfilm facilitated initial research on this study in 1955 and 1956. More recently a grant from the Alumni Research Fund of Clemson University expedited the reworking and publication of the book.

Although the financial asssistance of the Southern Fellowships Fund, Emory University, and Clemson University was vital to the effort within these pages, so indeed was the help of many individuals. To Dr. Bell I. Wiley of Emory University, who directed the dissertation which was the basis of this study, go my sincere thanks for his wise guidance and unfailing kindness. Dr. Virginia Bardsley of Clemson University made sound suggestions as to style changes in selected chapters.

My parents, the late Mary Beard and Thomas Harrison Spencer, were unstinting in their support. They, along with Mrs. Frances Witty Smith and the late Mr. Sydney A. Smith of Jackson, Mississippi, and Mr. and Mrs. Rabun Neal Patrick of Atlanta, Georgia, supplied the sustaining loyalty without which the project might not have survived. Dr. Jack K. Williams, former Vice-President and Dean of Faculty, Clemson University, now Commissioner of Higher Education for the State of Texas, merits gratitude for his consistent encouragement of and aid in the research and financing. The many librarians and archivists in state universities and archives are too numerous for individual acknowledgement, but their gracious assistance everywhere expedited research.

And finally, I deeply appreciate the careful work of Dr. Hugh H. Macaulay, Professor of Economics, and Mr. Jerome

V. Reel, Assistant Professor of History, Clemson University, who unselfishly undertook the wearisome task of proof reading.

MAY SPENCER RINGOLD

Department of Social Sciences
Clemson University

★

I

THE NEW ORDER

IN THE SIX WEEKS preceding the launching of the Confederate States of America, a new order began in the South. South Carolina, Mississippi, Florida, Alabama, Georgia, Louisiana, and Texas, through delegates in secession conventions, initially sought individual secession from the United States.

Political leadership in these states had publicized the rationale of secession in governors' messages and legislative resolutions or reports. In each state a secession convention proclaimed its justification in finely-phrased ordinances or declarations. An oft-reiterated theme was the threat posed by Republicans to equality of the states in all political rights and privileges. An oft-stated purpose was to obtain, outside the Federal Union, certain ends of government which the Constitution of the United States once guaranteed and which, in the thinking of secessionists, the action of non-slaveholding states now imperiled.[1]

As other slave states hesitated, Fort Sumter and Lincoln's call for troops strengthened separation sentiment within their borders, and four of these states followed their Southern sisters out of the Union. The newly-formed Confederacy completed its roster with the secession of Virginia, Arkansas, North Carolina, and Tennessee. As J. G. Randall put it, the secession of the upper South "followed as a result of the appeal to arms. . . . It was the question of 'which side.' "[2]

Eleven Southern states now had acted upon the right of revolution. For under the verbiage of ordinances or declara-

1

tions or resolutions, behind the peaceful withdrawal from the Union, there was cool determination in all seceding states to "alter, reform or abolish their government in such manner as they may think proper."[3]

The last four seceding states found a custom-made government waiting. On February 4, 1861, the new republics had coalesced. The confederated states had adopted a constitution then which combined guarantees of state sovereignty with the tried strength of federal polity. The constitution quite logically acknowledged the "sovereign and independent character" of the Confederate States. Constitutional provisions regarding taxation failed to include "general welfare" and made it, by implication, a state function. In such a scheme of things state officials retained the new dignity that their independent republics had conferred upon them. State legislatures incurred new responsibilities and unprecedented significance attached to their policies and programs. And for a time general assemblies had to share with secession conventions authority to declare the will of electorates and to implement their purposes.

The chaotic interlude between South Carolina's secession and that of the four border slave states had witnessed more than a foreshadowing of future developments in the South. Secessionist zeal of governors, state legislators, and convention delegates had to be translated into a mode of practical, political action. Amid mixed reactions and emphases, a certain pattern of organization became discernible.

Perhaps the chief aim characterizing action in each state was that of establishing the state as sovereign. The method of expressing this aim within the limits of constitutional form fell to the lot of men whose purposes and capacities were to be affected by the necessity of the war emergency that ensued. In fact, there was hardly time for an orderly metamorphosis. The viable organisms of state that appeared, marked as they were by inheritance, exhibited both affirmation and negation of the past and underwent inevitable alteration in the face of swift-paced events.

Separate sovereignty and subsequent confederation required adjustments in organic and statutory law. State con-

stitutions underwent revisions, with references to the United
States deleted and official oaths and treason laws changed.
Federal laws and Federal agencies affecting commerce, com-
munications, and the courts were on the one hand abro-
gated and on the other adapted to state and Confederate
jurisdiction.

Louisiana affords a typical picture. Three days after secession the Louisiana convention ordered that all Federal
officers connected with civil service in the state and all laws
relating to them should continue in force under state jurisdiction. Revenue and collection laws of the United States
became state laws. United States statutes concerning the circuit and district courts in Louisiana were "reenacted and
declared to be in full force and effect as laws of the State
of Louisiana." Postal employees functioned as state officials
until "otherwise ordered by convention or other authority."[4]

United States property—real estate, forts, arsenals, light-
houses, specie—was considered fair game by state governors
and conventions. The Texas convention ordered immediate
seizure of United States property.[5] Governors in the other
states of the Confederacy anticipated convention approval
in demanding surrender of Federal property. In every
instance conventions or legislatures sustained their action.
Seceding states having public domain land within borders
claimed title to the land.[6] Several states found it necessary
to pass measures looking to state control over Indians and
Indian reservations.[7]

Secession, then, involved more than negation of Federal
powers, offices, property rights, and authority, for almost
every voided Federal power had to be replaced by state or
Confederate activity. State governors, legislatures, or conventions had to fill the vacuum left by Southern rejection
of Federal authority.

A letter to the governor of Tennessee reveals in part a
new attitude toward gubernatorial duties.

For the first time, in the history of the State to be Governor
means something. Here-to-fore the position has been simply
nominal. . . . But *now*, how bold the contrast: With the liberties
of more than a million of people to maintain—our fields to pro-

tect, and the sanctity of our household Gods to preserve. . . .
Indeed we may exclaim to be Governor of the Commonwealth
at this time *means something*.[8]

Months before the governorship of Tennessee had come to
"mean something," other states had taken steps to strengthen
the authority of their executives.

The South Carolina convention had vested in the governor such duties as formerly came within the purview of
the president: the power to receive ambassadors, ministers,
consuls, and agents from foreign powers; to appoint foreign
agents; to make treaties with the consent of the senate; to
nominate for senate approval ambassadors and other officers.[9]
Other conventions and legislatures conferred additional
appointive powers on their governors. Executive councils
and military boards made their appearance as advisory committees to assist the governors.[10]

Even so, law-makers could not keep abreast of the formidable problems which governors were to face amid the
progressive disruption of Southern society and economy.
Governors were forced to try experimental schemes, with
or without legislative sanction, in order to combat recurring
homefront crises. Governor Henry Watkins Allen of
Louisiana established state stores to provide civilian necessities. Governor Zebulon Baird Vance of North Carolina
sent state-owned ships past blockading squadrons to bring
home supplies for military and domestic use. Joseph Emerson Brown of Georgia worked tirelessly and often dicta-
torially to alleviate the suffering of indigent civilians and
to clothe and feed Georgia troops. From executive offices
throughout the South a host of state purchasing agents
fanned out to Europe, to the West Indies, to Mexico, and
to sister states—bartering, borrowing, haggling, competing
with one another and with Confederate agents.

Legislative as well as executive departments faced un-
familiar tasks. Six states recognized the expanding scope of
legislative responsibility by requiring regular annual sessions.[11] States which retained the biennial system throughout
secession and the war found it expedient to have numerous

called meetings. North Carolina, for example, held seven extra or adjourned sessions of its general assembly; Mississippi and Texas legislators met in five called sessions; and in 1863 South Carolina saw reason to convene its law-makers three times in addition to the annual session of that year.[12]

Changing circumstances caused concern regarding the caliber of legislative personnel. Need for "wise heads" more than ever before was the subject of considerable editorial comment.[13] As the problems before state and Confederate governments became progressively harder to solve, public regard for legislative personnel ran the gamut from hopefulness to waning enthusiasm to disappointment, if not downright contempt. The Texas *State Gazette* expressed a sentiment in 1861 that had echoes throughout the South. After commenting on political novices in the legislature, it continued:

But it remains to be tested whether these new legislators will come up with clear and enlightened views as to the nature of the revolution . . . and the stupendous results . . . which must arise upon the foundations which will be laid by the Legislation of the ensuing twelve months.[14]

Observers of legislators began to express doubts as to their efficiency as early as 1861 and 1862. Time and again legislative loquacity and obsession with the trivial and purely political were criticized. An Alabama commentator complained that progress in legislation was slowed down by the irrepressible disposition of members to make speeches.[15] The Raleigh *Standard* accused the "Destructives" of wasting time.[16] The Nashville *Patriot* regretted that Tennessee legislators adjourned for a week to visit their families and to participate in the fall elections in 1861.[17] A New Orleans paper in December, 1861, ridiculed buffoonery in the Tennessee general assembly and suggested that it was high time for that body to adjourn.[18] A Virginia diarist bitterly resented the two months wasted by his state's general assembly in "wretched squabbles over the senatorship."[19]

William Gilmore Simms wrote of South Carolina lawmakers of 1861-1862: "The Legislature is reported to be the feeblist body known here for fifty years. There are some 96 new members, each eager to fire off his popgun at Convention & Council."[20] Another South Carolinian longed for the Calhouns, McDuffies, Turnbulls, Haynes, and Hugers of other days. "What has become of this race of men? Unless we can send better men to our next legislature, God only knows how we shall grope our way out of our many difficulties."[21]

Some of the criticism was unreasonable and unjustified, and the lawmakers, especially in the initial years, were not without defenders. The Montgomery *Mail* spoke highly of the state solons in 1862.[22] A Mississippi legislator, perhaps facetiously, found his colleagues at least "respectable in appearance."[23] The Texas *State Gazette* observed many "eminent" lawyers and several "distinguished" doctors on the floors of the Texas general assembly in 1861 and reported that those best acquainted with the legislative bodies of Texas in past years considered the incumbents "in point of industry, sobriety and general decorum . . . the superior of any body of the kind which has met in the State."[24] The Florida *Sentinel* in December, 1862, was "very favorably impressed with the House. . . . We don't think that there has been a buncombe speech made in the House—no speaking against time—no parliamentary shifts or devices."[25] Again in 1863 the paper complimented the recent legislature in these terms: "We know of no better working Body than the last general Assembly for many years past."[26]

The Raleigh *State Journal* in 1861 cautioned against too much fault-finding on the part of the public with legislative programs. "No doubt some unnecessary and unwise laws have been enacted," said this newspaper, "but there is also not a doubt that under all the circumstances, they did the best they could and that, from what has been done, much good will result in the end to the State."[27] A member of the North Carolina assembly wrote to his wife in 1862 saying, "The Legislature is giting along pretty well—we have perfected more legislation than at any previous session in the same time since I was a member of this body."[28]

It was generally true, however, that by 1863 lack of con-

fidence in legislative capacity to solve war-time problems
was widespread and increasing. A number of factors had
arisen by that time to create or intensify partisan dissensions
on the state level and thus to weaken morale. Social, economic, and political disorganization attendant on invasion,
on controversial Confederate policies, and on vitiating
defeatism had nourished disruptive tendencies throughout
the South. The Montgomery *Mail* believed that the election
of 1863 in Alabama inaugurated a "regular demagogical
reign, while the attention of more patriotic men was directed
to the efforts to drive the enemy from the country."[29] C. C.
Clay, of the same state, wrote Senator Louis T. Wigfall in
September, 1863, that the new general assembly had elected
its own officers and chosen a senator in William Lowndes
Yancey's place from men of Unionist stripe.[30]

Whig partisanship was attributed to the Georgia legislature of 1861.[31] But Governor Brown's hostility to the
Confederate administration was the key factor in promoting
antagonistic alignments among Georgia's legislators. By 1865
the *Countryman* was warning voters not to be duped by the
"delusive cry of 'no party.' " The last legislature was characterized as including "the most violent and bigoted party
men."[32]

The Raleigh *Semi-Weekly Register* laid party dissension
in the North Carolina legislature squarely at the door of
William W. Holden, whom it accused of organizing a conservative party.[33] Holden attributed conservative participation to the proscription of Unionists who had joined secessionists after Lincoln's call to arms. The secessionists, Holden
contended, had usurped prominent positions; and they were,
in his opinion, "incompetent men—blustering party hacks."
In time the former Unionists had reasserted their earlier
influence; and the people of North Carolina had upheld
them.[34] It is impossible to determine the relative validity of
Holden's claims and those of his opponents. A majority of
North Carolinians would probably have subscribed to the
opinion registered by the Wilmington *Journal* concerning
the legislature of 1863: "We hardly think that the State ever
did have precisely such another Legislature. Are we singular

in expressing the hope that it may never again have another exactly like it?"[35]

Partisan conflicts in general assemblies were naturally viewed with distaste by a citizenry so desperately in need of judicious legislation. There is also some evidence that the conduct of legislators in the face of Federal invasion enhanced public disesteem. An anonymous commentator gave the following description of Tennessee lawmakers during the evacuation of Nashville:

Messengers had been sent around to hurry up the laggard members, and as those who were present strolled about "from pillow to post," from door to window, eagerly gazing for the appearance of some fellow-member so as to get a quorum, their faces presented the most interesting study we have ever beheld in human nature. . . . Anxiety and fear struggled for the mastery; where the latter had manifestly asserted its supremacy, that "pallor which sets upon the brow of death" was but too visible where the ruddy glow of excellent satisfaction was marked the day before. . . . It is said the members of the Legislature presented rather a ludicrous appearance as they trudged off towards the depot of one or the other of the railroads, each one with a trunk on his back or carpet sack and bundle in hand.[36]

The Virginia legislature seems to have acquitted itself creditably during the invasion threat of 1862.[37] But in 1864 when Sherman's army turned toward Milledgeville, the Georgia legislature behaved very much like the Tennessee assembly of 1862. A Milledgeville girl who witnessed the panic gave the following report of it in her diary:

The Scene at the State House was truly ridiculous, the members were badly scared. Such a body of representatives make my cheeks glow with shame. What a time it was for the display of cool, wise, legislation and undaunted courage and exalted patriotism, instead of that they passed a law levying troops *en masse,* excepting the legislators and judiciary. [Two] paid three thousand dollars for the conveyance to move with speed from this place of danger.[38]

The Harris County *Enterprise* in describing the same event said:

For shame, gentlemen! What a burlesque upon patriotism. We feel humbled—humiliated—in the sight of the people of our sister States of the Confederacy that the representatives of the great state of Georgia should act in such a manner.[39]

For varying periods of time and to varying degrees, conventions vied with legislatures and governors in directing state affairs. Several state conventions were indeed secession conventions, making only those adjustments to separation and confederation which the new order demanded. The Mississippi convention acknowledged priority of the general assembly by conceding the right of the latter to repeal ordinances except those dissolving the Union and effecting constitutional changes.[40] In Alabama the convention accepted the principle of legislative repeal of ordinances except for those ordinances incorporated into the constitution.[41] The Georgia convention held sacrosanct from legislative repeal the ordinance of secession, ratification of the Confederate Constitution, ordinances relative to the state constitution, relations with other states and measures which by their own terms would require convention action.[42] Harmony prevailed in Texas convention-legislature relations. According to an "Address to the People of Texas," drafted by Pryor Lea, John Henry Brown and John D. Stell, the convention "proceeded to do whatever the occasion required; but no more." It created a temporary Committee of Public Safety to cope with the evacuation of the United States army in the state and to arrange for frontier protection when that force was withdrawn. It provided for continuity of civil government when Governor Sam Houston and his secretary of state refused to take the oath of allegiance to the Confederate constitution. Its labours done on March 25, it confided "in that body [the state legislature] and the present Executive and Judiciary, to conduct the State government according to the will and interests of their constituents."[43]

But accord between conventions and legislatures was by no means routine. The Louisiana convention allegedly constituted itself the "governing power" from the time of the state's secession to the state's ratification of the Confederate constitution.[44] The New Orleans *Daily True Delta* reported

the state legislature as "virtually dead" in February, 1861.[45]
The Baton Rouge *Daily Advocate* condoned the "local character of legislative acts as arising from convention consideration of matters heretofore under the guardianship of the
Legislature."[46] Early adjournment *sine die* of the Louisiana
Convention, March 26, 1861, put an end to discussion of its
authority.

The Florida convention, which met in four sessions, the
last in February, 1862, gave Governor John Milton some
trouble. It consistently sought to restrain expenditures and
disbanded the militia. Milton's repeated efforts to recon-
stitute a militia system were unsuccessful until 1864, and
Florida's protection from the enemy was left to Confederate
troops. In this state the convention had strong supporters
among whom were Milton S. Perry, ex-Governor, and the
editor of the Florida *Sentinel*.[47] The *Sentinel* defended
reassembling the convention in 1862 and urged that it
create an executive council which would assist the governor
and act as a check upon his authority.[48] A letter written by
Governor Milton in February, 1862, claimed state-wide disapproval of what he regarded as convention dictatorship.[49]

In the early months of 1861, Virginia secessionists had
attacked their convention. The Richmond *Examiner* ridiculed the convention as weak, composed of old men who
knew nothing but law and who were capable of no other
pursuit.[50] One critic, waxing impatient at the convention's
reluctance to secede, referred to the delegates as "those old
fossils at Richmond."[51] As the convention dragged into the
summer, its personnel faced accusations of self-seeking, ex-
travagance and political intrigue. The *Examiner* saw in the
body's final session of December, 1861, another attempt to
usurp the power of the Virginia legislature, which was shortly
to assemble.[52]

The South Carolina convention included men of recognized stature. The respect accorded its membership brought
into relief the legislators' reputation for inefficiency.[53] Here,
as in Florida, friction developed between governor and convention over the nature of the executive council. A new

council had replaced the first cabinet in December, 1861. The new group consisted of five members: the governor, lieutenant-governor and three councilors chosen by the convention. It was not responsible to the governor and it wielded extraordinary power.[54] Governor Francis W. Pickens opposed its creation. David Flavel Jamison in a letter of March, 1862, tried to convince the governor that the new council represented a "concentration and condemnation of the power of the convention, so far as the prompt exercise of extraordinary powers might be required. . . . So far from a disparagement of your position it effects . . . an elevation and gives you higher powers."[55] Friends of Pickens joined him in opposition to the executive board, however, and conspired to destroy it. Opposition to the convention found its way facilitated by the very energy and efficiency of the council in dealing with the controversial problems of conscription, impressment and supply. Public antipathy toward both the council and convention resulted in the passage of an ordinance providing for the expiration of the convention on December 17, 1862. The legislature in December of the same year brought the executive council to an end.[56]

The North Carolina convention assembled four times. Three of these sessions occurred after the extra legislature adjourned in September, 1861, and before the regular general assembly met in November, 1862. During that time, the convention served as a lawmaking body, controlled by "elderly men who were mainly Whigs and Unionists."[57] To such conservatives as Jonathan Worth this situation was highly desirable because of the ability, efficiency, and economy of the convention as compared with the legislature. Worth expressed the hope that the convention would continue to supplant the legislature throughout the war.[58] The Raleigh *Standard* gave consistent support to the convention.[59] On the other hand, the Wilmington *Daily Journal* was already in June, 1861, wondering: "When will it adjourn!"[60] In the extra session of the legislature which met in August and September, 1862, antagonism was keen and bitter. A young soldier writing in November said:

The State Convention meets today. I intend to go in tomorrow and see what kind of a monster this legislatorial bugbear is (for to read the speeches delivered on the floor of the Legislature it were a bugbear indeed, at which the stoutest Blackstone would quail) .[61]

An influential member of the North Carolina convention believed that the efforts to discredit that body's policies arose from the convention's determination to equalize taxation upon slaves as upon other property.[62] Be that as it may, support of the convention could not offset opposition. When Governor Zebulon Vance urged calling the convention to deal with extortion and speculation in the fall of 1862, the president of the convention felt it wise to decline.[63] The future guidance of North Carolina's destiny became the sole responsibility of the governor and elected legislators.[64] After 1862, throughout the states of the Southern Confederacy, governors and legislators unaided by debatable convention assistance were to grapple with ever-mounting obstacles to internal security and stability. Indeed, the confederated states were to find adjustment to the new order increasingly complicated as invasion bit deeper and deeper into the South.

★

II

LOCAL DEFENSE

ONE ASPECT OF ADJUSTMENT to the new order received
immediate attention in all Southern states. Prevailing
opinion demanded creation of local defense units. This
attitude arose from something more than adherence to
theories of state sovereignty. It sprang from realities incident
to the negation of Federal authority, to the vastness of the
new nation, and to the make-up of its people.

Before the Confederacy was established, state authorities
had brought most of the Federal forts and arsenals under
their control. The secession of Texas and, later, Arkansas
left western frontiers bereft of Federal safeguards against
hostile Indians. Furthermore, the Confederacy sprawled
over about seven hundred and fifty thousand square miles
with its long line of inadequately defended border and
coast inviting Union raids. Not the least formidable of the
realities which the South confronted were the presence of
over three million Negroes and resultant fears of slave
revolt.[1]

Conventions and legislatures relied for a time on volunteer defense forces, and Southerners manifested great zeal
in 1861 for state service. By March, South Carolina could
boast of 104 companies organized into ten regiments, four
brigades and one division.[2] The volunteer army in Mississippi swelled in May to two hundred companies over and
above those requisitioned by the president of the Confederacy.[3]

The secession convention in Alabama set up machinery
for both three-year regulars and for volunteers to serve for

13

not less than one year. Departments of the adjutant general and quartermaster general in the regular and volunteer armies were distinct from corresponding departments in the militia.[4] Georgia had earlier established the office of adjutant and inspector general with specific duties affecting militia and volunteer units and had prepared for possible war by outlining the framework for a volunteer army of ten thousand.[5]

In Virginia the local defense system had the distinction of being organized by Robert E. Lee, who served as major-general of Virginia. The convention in Virginia planned to use a volunteer and a regular army. Difficulties in recruiting three-year regulars simultaneously with one-year volunteers led to the abandonment of the regular forces.[6]

North Carolina's legislature authorized a force of ten thousand to serve the state during the war.[7] Questioning the wisdom of maintaining an expensive defense system, the convention ordered discharge of all volunteers not requisitioned by the president.[8] When the legislature convened again in August, 1861, it suspended the convention ordinance and permitted the governor to accept as many as eleven thousand volunteers for the war.[9] Tennessee laws regarding volunteer forces were more optimistic as to manpower resources than those of neighboring North Carolina. The legislature in May, 1861, created on paper an army of fifty-five thousand.[10]

In Texas and Arkansas the first legislation governing state forces was designed to protect the frontier against Indians. The Texas Convention and legislature organized one regiment for twelve months and later created a ranger corps subject to Confederate regulation, but not removable from the state.[11]

Confederate requisitions for state troops in 1861 and Confederate conscription in 1862 decimated state forces. South Carolina had no army at all by early 1863 except for the Combahe Rangers and two cavalry companies.[12] When Charles Clark became governor of Mississippi in 1863, he demanded that the Confederacy leave him the one state brigade then unattached to the Confederate army.[13] The

Florida convention disbanded those state forces that were not transferred to Confederate service and hopefully entrusted its safety to the central government.[14] Louisiana, on the other hand, sought to entice volunteers into state units by offering a $50 bounty for each private and non-commissioned officer and an eighty-acre grant of land at the end of the war.[15] Virginia tried for a time to maintain an army of ten thousand non-conscripts for defense of the state west of the Blue Ridge. After Confederate conscription had come to include this "State Line," the legislature proposed recalling and dismissing the army.[16]

Considerable controversy occurred in late 1862 and early 1863 over the passage of a ten-regiment bill in North Carolina. One proposal would have permitted the governor to raise troops using men between the ages of eighteen and forty-five not liable to Confederate draft. Another would empower the governor to accept volunteers subject to conscription but not already in the Confederate service. The North Carolina *Register* and the Wilmington *Journal* opposed the latter bill because of potential conflict with the Confederate administration; and the measure failed of passage at the time.[17]

As the Confederate army swallowed up the volunteers, states came to concern themselves with substantial revision of militia systems. North Carolina altered her militia laws in September, 1861, after a portion of her coast had suffered invasion.[18] South Carolina in the same year tightened control over her manpower by subjecting all males, sixteen to sixty, to patrol duty and providing for their rapid mobilization into state service if necessary.[19] The Alabama legislature contented itself with ordering more frequent district and county musters; and Texas took steps to create thirty-three militia brigades.[20] The Virginia militia regulations of 1861 were perhaps the most realistic in that they provided for an active corp composed of men from twenty-one to thirty-one years of age, and a reserve militia.[21]

Mississippi, Tennessee, and Louisiana were somewhat tardy in revamping their militia laws. A Mississippi bill of early 1862 increased militia efficiency by ordering a new enrollment of white males, eighteen through fifty years of age. The Governor could draft these enrollees to fill Confederate requisitions and meet emergencies within the state.[22] Governor John Jones Pettus made full use of his powers and employed his militia in bolstering Mississippi River defenses after the fall of Memphis and New Orleans in 1862.[23]

Louisiana militia legislation of 1862 was moderate, subjecting men from eighteen through forty-five to active service for three months or, in cases of urgent necessity, for as long as six months.[24] With Tennessee on the very brink of disaster in March, 1862, the general assembly of that state ordered the organization of men between eighteen and forty-five into reserve military corps. Men between forty-five and fifty-five were to be subject to call only after the younger group had been utilized; and they could not be detailed, transferred, or drafted into Confederate service.[25]

Florida and Georgia legislatures and conventions refused early in the war to reform the militia system. Florida's governor, Milton Perry, had been successful before the war in obtaining changes; but the reforms had produced indifferent results.[26] Governor Perry and his successor John Milton unsuccessfully advocated stringent legislation for home defense.[27] Milton wrote in 1862 that no organization of militia existed, ". . . and there are so few liable to military duty, in the several districts or beats, that no organization can be made agreeably to the provisions of the Statutes of the State."[28]

Georgia limped along through 1861 and 1862 with her old pre-war system in spite of the governor's request for a new law.[29] The situation was reversed in Arkansas, where an act modernizing the militia was killed by the governor's veto.[30] Arkansas was described as "utterly undefended" in 1862, with such militia companies as did exist "badly organized and poorly armed."[31]

Voices occasionally were heard urging the wisdom of adequately training manpower of the states for local defense and condemning legislatures for their lack of foresight. The Richmond *Daily Examiner* questioned the ability of the general assembly to enact such a measure and described it as a "body of county courts and cross-roads electioneers," now called upon to devise a "measure distasteful to influential citizens of the country and necessarily unpopular."[32] An Alabamian writing to his governor complained that there was not an officer "of any grade" in his part of the county.[33]

Confederate requisitions and conscriptions in time forced legislatures to consider the training of men left at home. The South Carolina executive council salvaged for militia duty men sixteen through sixty not in the Confederate army.[34] Later the legislature of that state gave the governor authority to appoint enrolling officers in each judicial district to list for duty all men between eighteen and forty-five.[35] The governor could order militia to other states provided it remained under his control.[36]

The invasion of Mississippi prompted the legislature in December, 1863, to lower the age limit for militia to seventeen and to subject to militia service men exempted or discharged by Confederate authorities. Further alterations in the law revised the age limits downward to sixteen and upward to fifty-five.[37]

Walter L. Fleming, referring to conditions in the militia in Alabama in 1862, said: "The fact was, there was no longer any militia; the officers and men had gone, or were preparing to go, into the Confederate service."[38] Although letters in the Alabama governors' papers indicate that musters still occurred in some areas regularly, need for reform was obvious.[39] Governor John Gill Shorter in August, 1863, persuaded the Alabama legislature to strengthen the militia law. The new system divided men into two categories: those under seventeen and over forty-five formed the first-class militia and served only in their home counties. The second-class militia included men between seventeen and forty-five years of age who had been exempted by Confederate authorities. According to some accounts, this militia was effective only for "local defense and for executing the state laws in particular localities."[40]

Texas tried several expedients in 1863 to render its militia more effective. The general assembly set up a draft system to obtain from militia companies state troops requisitioned

by the president to cooperate with Confederate commanders.[41] A Louisiana refugee reported the law as most unpopular and said that "Unionism is rampant about here. . . .
Half of the militia have been drafted for six months, and
oh, the moaning and bewailing of the feminine population."[42] In order to insure a fair distribution of the burden
of active militia service, the legislature divided the militia
into three classes to serve in turn.[43] As usual, objections to
the law were raised. The *Daily Telegraph* thought that the
men would be more useful at home and that the militia,
even when organized and called into service, actually added
very little to state defense.[44]

North Carolina, Louisiana, and Georgia legislatures attempted to work out more adequate militia laws in 1863.
Governor Vance of North Carolina received authority to
call for local and temporary service all males between
eighteen and forty-five.[45] The legislature later created a
home guard from members of the eighteen to fifty group
not in Confederate service and subject to the same exemptions as those provided by militia regulations and acts of the
Confederate congress.[46]

Louisiana laws embraced men from seventeen through
fifty for service of six months or as long as necessary.[47] The
measures did not meet with a happy response on the part
of citizenry. In May, Adjutant General C. le D. Elgee re-
signed his position with the state, giving as one of his reasons
that the law was "universally execrated" and that the adjutant general "can do but little good."[48] When Henry Watkins
Allen became governor in January, 1864, he asked for and
received a new militia law. In his opinion the old legislation failed for want of enforcement provisions.[49]

The Georgia legislature acceded in 1863 to the governor's
request for a modernized militia measure. Each senatorial
district became a separate militia district in which men from
sixteen through sixty were enrolled. Enrollees were divided
into two classes, those from seventeen through fifty forming
the militia proper; and those sixteen to seventeen and fifty
to sixty comprising a reserve corps. The governor could fill
requisitions from the president for state troops by apportion-

ing a draft among regiments; and battalions could be formed, if necessary, without regard for county lines or senatorial districts.[50] During the crisis of late 1864, Governor Brown requested a law providing for a *levy en masse*. The legislature on the same day gave him authority to summon to service the "entire white male population" of the state, with certain reservations, between the ages of sixteen and sixty-five.[51]

Governor John Milton of Florida had repeatedly sought revised laws for local defense. A letter from Governor Milton to General Richard F. Floyd told of the governor's chagrin at his helpless situation. "The General Assembly refused, tho' frequently and earnestly urged by me, to enact any law authorizing the organization of the militia, or state forces of any kind, or, to provide any means of defence [sic] for the State."[52] The governor's efforts finally met with legislative cooperation in December, 1864, when the legislature passed a measure calling for the enrollment of all men ineligible for the Confederate States' service, sixteen through fifty-five. The governor was to arm this force and to keep it in readiness to serve any Confederate commander who should call upon the governor for aid.[53]

The recalcitrance of the Virginia legislators toward militia reform brought condemnation from their governor.[54] By 1864, however, the Richmond *Enquirer* was doubting the judgment of the governor. This newspaper felt that non-conscripts could best be used in the production of foodstuff.[55]

All the Southern states limited militia efficiency by generous exemption policies. The tendency to increase exemptions from militia duty did not result altogether from pressure exerted by special interests groups. On the contrary, exemption laws indicate an attempt to keep open as nearly as possible avenues of trade, transportation, and communication; to maintain as nearly as possible business as usual under war-time conditions.

In the first two years of war legislatures in South Carolina, Mississippi, Alabama, Louisiana, and Virginia began to release men of certain professions and trades involving war production from militia obligation.[56] Throughout the South a substantial increase in the numbers and categories of exemptions from militia service appeared in 1863. In many instances this reflected a continuing effort to husband labor for needed production.[57] But inequities persisted. Family physicians tended to be lax in certifying to physical infirmities. The burden of militia duty fell heavily on the farming population. And the fact that scores of state and county officials escaped service tended to enhance distrust of the system among many people in all the states.[58]

Not only did the out-dated militia laws in the South in 1861 give evidence of lack of planning ahead for war, but sovereign status also caught the seceding states deficient in materiel of war. The situation in Virginia was typical of conditions elsewhere. As one legislator put it:

> She is as defenceless [sic] as a helpless child. . . . The State has *no* arms of modern structure & none to meet a formidable enemy such as we may anticipate in the event of collision. It will take several months, perhaps 6 or more to purchase & get at home the arms we are obliged to have even to *commence* warfare.[59]

Legislatures and conventions began in 1861 to fill the need in various ways. In South Carolina and Virginia, boards of ordnance for a time took over the responsibility of purchasing supplies, allocating arms, and if necessary supervising the manufacture of materiel.[60] During the existence of the Texas convention a Committee of Public Safety began to accumulate arms and ammunition.[61] Its duties were later transferred to a military board. Mississippi, North Carolina, Arkansas, Louisiana, and Tennessee divided the burdens of supply for the armies in 1861 between governors and military boards, and in some instances ordnance departments and special commissions.[62] Florida, Georgia, and Alabama relied largely on their governors to procure necessary arms, ammunition, and provisions.

Equipping troops for state volunteer armies and for the Confederacy produced severe shortages in the South. The stockpiles hastily acquired by purchase, by seizure of Federal forts and arsenals, and by contributions from enthusiastic Southerners had dwindled alarmingly by the late summer and early fall of 1861. State governors were beginning to feel a need to reserve remaining stores for local defense.[63]

The South Carolina convention sought to solve the dilemma by creating an executive council with extraordinary powers including acquisition of war supplies. The chief of the military, James Chesnut, Jr., Lieutenant Governor W. W. Harllee and W. H. Gist, who headed the Departments of Treasury and Finance, worked rapidly, dispatching agents throughout the state to buy cotton for shipment abroad and agents to Europe to bargain there for supplies.[64] A separate department of construction and manufacture under the supervision of W. H. Gist established a state armory at Greenville, South Carolina. Major W. G. Eason of the State Ordnance Bureau wrote Governor Pickens in November, 1862, that workmen were busy repairing and altering old arms gathered throughout the state. He predicted that it would be some months before machinery would be in readiness for production.[65]

State legislatures authorized purchase of arms from individuals, collection of guns belonging to the state or the Confederacy in hands of persons not in service, and the repair and reconditioning of worn-out and discarded guns.[66] Institutions such as penitentiaries and schools for defectives became production centers for ammunition, uniforms, tents, and other equipment for the armed forces.[67]

Governor Francis Richard Lubbock of Texas urged the legislature to place the securities of the state at the disposal of some agent to finance purchases of defense materiel.[68] An act of his legislature gave the governor $500,000 in bonds and a military board with which to work.[69] The first military board in Texas faced difficulties in the sale of bonds, a scarcity of transportation facilities, and competition for purchase of the cotton used in payment for contracts.[70] Among its accomplishments were the cap and cartridge factory in the Supreme Court building and a cannon factory in Austin.[71] A new military board created in 1863 took over control of all public works and supplies and the importation of articles needed.[72]

North Carolina and Alabama tried by subsidies to encourage production of needed supplies. A North Carolina law offered a bounty of $10,000 in the form of a loan or stock subscription to any company establishing a powder mill, and at the same time the bill gave approval to state agencies for powder production. The North Carolina Powder Manufacturing Company took immediate advantage of the law.[73]

When Governor Vance took office, he approached the problem of supply directly and dramatically. Without legislative authority, Vance sent John White as purchasing agent to Europe and negotiated for the purchase of a vessel by the state for transportation of state-imported goods.[74] Vance had begun to implement his ideas in January, 1863; and in its next session the legislature gave sanction to his program. The general assembly appropriated $324,000 in December, 1863, to enable the governor to purchase cotton to be applied on the state's account in Europe.[75] The legislature later appointed a blockade commissioner.[76]

The state project met with some objection. Jonathan Worth observed:

We raise money in Europe under the disadvantage always attaching to a borrower of doubtful credit—buy with gold thus obtained and sell what costs us a dollar in gold for four dollars in Confederate currency, the four dollars being worth about 20 cents in the currency we pay. This is speculation with a vengeance. . . .[77]

Despite such criticism, the consensus was favorable because the system worked to the advantage of North Carolina troops.

Georgia followed North Carolina's example and entered the export-import business to obtain war materiel and consumer goods. The legislature allowed the governor $750,000 initially for the purpose and gave him authority to purchase a "good swift steamer."[78] Brown chartered four vessels instead. When Confederate regulations restricted the trade, controversy ensued. A compromise policy exempted state-owned vessels from the Confederate regulations; whereupon Brown entered, allegedly, into a bogus purchase of a vessel with Gazaway B. Lamar, which proved to be of temporary advantage to both the state and the Lamar business interests.[80]

Had fortune permitted the Confederacy to develop its machinery of government under peaceful conditions, the efforts of Southern states to muster and to supply forces for local defense might have followed the pattern of inertia which characterized ante-bellum militia systems. But war enormously complicated the problems attendant upon the central government's ordeal of initial organization and finance. States' authorities had cause to doubt the ability of the Confederacy to deploy strong units for frontier and border defense and to insure safety from slave insurrections. They had cause to question the soundness of the new government's credit in the market places of Europe from whence must come materiel of war. Under these circumstances, states' legislative leaders and governors keenly felt the need to mobilize, to maintain, and to supply state forces—volunteer or regular states' armies or militia. This compulsion to give citizens such armed protection as the states could provide would, in time, inevitably dig into Confederate manpower and materiel potential. It is true that in the wild enthusiasm of early 1861 for secession and confederation and war Southern states' authorities surrendered men and war supplies to the Confederacy enthusiastically. Even then, however, they evinced a reluctance to strip their states. And it was not long before this reluctance hardened, among some Southern leaders, into obstruction of Confederate military policies.

III

CONFEDERATE-STATE RELATIONS

"How long shall the doctrine of State rights, so confident of its approved strength, be able to suppress its disorganizing instincts? The answer is patent: until a day or an hour furnish a provocation or a temptation."[1] Thus in 1864 did C. C. S. Farrar point up the cleavage between state and Confederate interests. And historians of the Confederacy down to the present have focused attention upon those "disorganizing instincts" of state rights. They have spotlighted the recalcitrants among governors and other state politicians, giving weight to the obstructionist tendencies which certainly existed.

Yet the Confederate Congress and the Confederate administration were as thoroughly imbued with state rights doctrines as were local leaders. Indeed it is ironical that in passing legislation which required implementation at the state level, the Confederate Congress gave to state rights its first "provocation" or "temptation." Among this legislation were the acts creating a Confederate army, the first of which authorized the president to receive troops tendered by states or volunteers with the consent of the governors.[2] Letters from the War Department to states' governors specifying local quotas elicited cordial response, initially, and state conventions and legislatures acted to promote compliance with Confederate needs.[3]

It is certainly true, however, that misunderstandings and disagreements on minor points occurred during the first hectic months of organization. Joseph Brown demanded the right to turn over parts of Georgia regiments with necessary officers and to continue feeding volunteers into the units until the regiments were complete. This concession would enable Georgia regiments to enter the provisional army with officers elected by their men and commissioned by Governor Brown. Brown further asked that his troops leaving for Pensacola be mustered into Confederate service before leaving the state. Both requests were contrary to Confederate policy. The issues were adjusted in time to the satisfaction of the secretary of war with Brown's reluctant acquiescence.[4]

Antagonism between several governors and the Confederate administration developed in May when an act of Congress changed enlistment practices, permitting the president to receive companies, battalions, and regiments without call upon state governors.[5] The Florida legislature criticized the act in a resolution condemning the new system as a "dangerous infraction of the rights of the sovereign states."[6] Governor Brown frustrated the effective operation of the act in Georgia by arming only those forces requisitioned through his office and by sending other companies off to Confederate service without state arms, ammunition, and accoutrement.[7] The North Carolina legislature gave its assent to direct tender of troops to the Confederacy, but it required officers to report to the governor the number and kind of such troops so that they might be counted among the state's quota.[8]

Further confusion resulted from conflicting Confederate orders as to term of enlistment. Word went out to several states in May, 1861, that twelve-month units would no longer be received. Governors were at the time in the process of forming twelve-month units for the Confederacy. It became necessary, then, to obtain the consent of the volunteers to serve throughout the war or to disband those already enlisted —ofttimes already in camp—who withheld consent to a longer term of service. After some vacillation, the Confederate war department determined to accept troops for twelve months if presented fully armed and equipped. "Troops armed and equipped by the Government must serve for the war."[9] The Mississippi legislature clarified its position regarding the term of enlistment by authorizing the transfer of volunteer companies in the state service to the Confederate army only with the consent of the men to such length of time as the "requisition may fix." Consent was not necessary if the troops were transferred for one year or less.[10] In other states the changes in Confederate enlistment practices bred resentment. Nevertheless, the Southern states during 1861 usually met and often surpassed demands made on them for men to muster into Confederate service. Military crises showed that state governments were also ready to give money and to lend state troops or militia in cooperation with the Confederate army in the field.

By the spring of 1862, however, General George B. McClellan's projected invasion of Virginia brought a new threat to the Confederacy. At this time many of the one-year volunteers were about to complete their enlistment period and thus present the possibility of a disintegrating Confederate army—a problem about which both state and Confederate leadership expressed concern.[11] The passage of the Confederacy's first conscription law solved the problem. But immediately carping critics attacked the law, although few failed to appreciate the necessity from which the law arose.[12] In the words of a Georgia humorist, the state through her legislature "ort to protess again the kornscript Ac, but go along and do it."[13]

There were several aspects of the conscription law that gave opportunity for conflict between Confederate and state authorities. One of these was the extent of state control over Confederate exemptions from service. James Chesnut of the South Carolina Executive Council thought that the Confederate conscription act would not render inoperative state certificates of exemption;[14] while the Florida attorney-general believed that those who held state offices created by state constitutions or those whose duties resulted from functions outlined in the constitutions would be exempted.[15]

The Confederate Congress clarified and extended exemption laws from time to time, but never to the satisfaction of all. *The Weekly Mississippian* urged that conscription include every able-bodied man in the Confederacy and that details from the army carry on necessary production.[16] The

Montgomery *Mail* believed the law inequitable since it favored certain professions and property without compelling exempted ones to contribute toward equalizing the burdens of war.[17] A resolution passed by the North Carolina legislature opposed the twenty-Negro law, which released one slave owner or overseer for every twenty slaves on farms or plantations.[18] Indeed, the twenty-Negro law was generally execrated.

In 1863 the Confederacy added to its lists of exemptions all officers whom state governors considered essential to the administration of state and local government. State legislatures in some instances specified the essential officials, and in other states left the matter to the discretion of their governors.

The most serious opposition to conscription came after the passage of the act of February 19, 1864, which drafted men from seventeen through fifty. Afterwards, state laws, which were extended to include exemption of minor state officials, reflected the general disapproval of the new Confederate policy. The Texas legislature took the position that no officer of a sovereign state could be placed in military service of the Confederacy without his consent.[19] North Carolina and Virginia general assemblies enacted similar measures.[20]

Georgia's governor, who had opposed conscription from the first, launched a formidable attack on the 1864 act in a called session of the general assembly.[21] At first he met with rebuff in the state legislature, and the legislators ordered him to interpose no obstacle to the enforcement of conscription.[22] When, in the last months of war, the Georgia legislature did pass a resolution asking for repeal of the conscription act and a return to the volunteer system, the move was apparently a sincere attempt to stay desertion and to build up Confederate forces.[23]

Although state laws gave at least lip-service cooperation to the Confederate government in its attempts to curtail desertion, further opportunity for friction between states and the Confederacy arose over methods of controlling the evil.

Mississippi laws required sheriffs to enroll all persons

subject to conscription and gave sheriffs the power to arrest deserters.[24] Later legislation enabled the Mississippi governor to use militia in arresting Confederate absentees and deserters.[25] Law-makers in Texas, North Carolina, and Georgia set penalties for aiding deserters.[26] Yet desertion was rife in the Confederate armies from 1862 to the end. Richard Harrison wrote the governor of Mississippi in December, 1862, that about one-half of the fighting strength of General John C. Pemberton's Mississippi contingent was absent without leave.[27] Apparently, states faced enforcement problems that were insurmountable. Local civil officials were sometimes negligent in their duties or in league with offenders.[28] State militia were little better. James Phelan of Mississippi described his state's militia as a "refuge for Confederate conscripts and deserters and naturally retained rather than returned its ill-gotten gains."[29]

Conscription could have been enforced and desertion controlled by the suspension of the writ of habaes corpus and the use of martial law, described by one historian of the Confederacy as the "most effective" method for insuring maximum effectiveness of conscription practices.[30] Congress tried the device and gave the president the power to suspend the right to the writ of habeas corpus from February 27 to October 13, 1862; from October 13, 1862, to February 13, 1863; and from February 15, 1864, to August 1, 1864. Although Davis's exercise of the power was never extensive, still the policy brought forth one of the most unpleasant of the crises between Confederate and States' authority. The clash which ensued was the first which found state legislatures almost solidly behind their governors in obstruction of Confederate policies.

The Florida legislature resolved that "the civil authority is the supreme and paramount power in this State." And in reiterating the doctrine of state rights in 1864, Florida emphasized the privilege of the writ of habeas corpus among the "cardinal principles of our free institutions."[31] In other states, legislation approximated nullification of the Confederate acts authorizing suspension of the writ.

The controversy over the habeas corpus measure reached

its peak in North Carolina and Georgia. Within these states political leaders eloquently and violently denounced suspension.[32] The North Carolina legislature in February, 1863, ordered the state's attorney general to the Salisbury Prison to sue out writs of habeas corpus for any North Carolina citizens there, if "proper and expedient." A North Carolina law instructed sheriffs to take into their custody any person unlawfully detained by Confederate authorities.[33] Supreme Court judges were permitted to grant writs of habeas corpus returnable before themselves, before any judge of the state, as well as before any other member of the state Supreme Court.[34] A joint committee of the North Carolina general assembly claimed that suspension was "unconstitutional, unnecessary, and dangerous." Its report also reversed the earlier, tacit acceptance of conscription.[35] A resolution against conscription and suspension of the writ of habeas corpus carried by a vote of sixty-seven to thirty-two.[36] The legislature followed up the censure by setting a fine of $1000 and imprisonment for not less than a year as punishment for failure to honor a writ.[37] Again in 1865, the North Carolina legislature defined the right of congress to authorize suspension as extending only to cases involving persons "who may stand committed for criminal or supposed criminal offences."[38]

Georgia's reaction paralleled that of North Carolina. Georgia laws of 1863 penalized judges and justices to the extent of a $2500 fine for refusal to honor writs. A resolution on the suspension within the Trans-Mississippi Military Department in 1864 excoriated the act as "an attempt . . . to give validity to unconstitutional seizures of the persons of the people."[39] Although such politicos as Robert Toombs, Alexander Stephens, and Governor Brown were fomenting the attack on the suspension of the writ, legislative opposition in Georgia was not unanimous. Forty-one members of the general assembly voted against the Linton Stephens' resolutions of censure.[40] And the *Countryman* expressed sorrow that the Georgia legislature had so little faith in the Confederate administration.[41]

Confederate laws affecting man-power for its armies had

involved dependence upon state action and had evoked both cooperation and conflict. So, indeed, did Confederate attempts to obtain arms, ammunition, and other supplies for its troops. Frank L. Owsley flayed state legislatures and governors for withholding munitions of war during the first and critical year. "Theoretically," he declared, "the states did transfer the arms and munitions captured with the United States arsenals, but in actual practice the several governors each disposed of a large part of those arms according to the interests of their respective states or according to their individual judgment." He continued, "As to the arms actually owned by the states, the governors either refused to allow them to be carried out of the state or gave them up reluctantly and sparingly."[42]

The Southern states in their sovereign and independent status had begun the task of accumulating arms, ammunition, and other defense materiel before the Confederacy came into being. After its organization the Confederate government lacked the resources needed to equip its armies. It asked for and received the war materiel captured from the United States government by the several states.[43] And when war became more than a probability, the central government received from the states not only the provisional forces, but also necessary equipment for those forces. The states, through legislatures or conventions, made ready to outfit volunteers for service with the Confederacy. Appeals went out from state capitals urging volunteers to bring their own arms to points of mobilization. County courts received authorization to levy taxes for equipping local companies. Military boards were ordered to "ration and subsist" volunteer companies. State agencies sprang up to handle supplies from private contribution.[44]

Governor Francis W. Pickens of South Carolina reported in July, 1861, that he had received 15,000 effective arms from the United States Arsenal and had purchased 11,000. With these arms he had supplied and sent soldiers to Virginia, Florida, Tennessee, and to the South Carolina defenses around Charleston. He stated that all the arms he could raise would be required to equip the last Confederate requisition for 3,000 men.[45] Governor Albert B. Moore of Alabama told his general assembly that he had followed the direction of the convention and turned over to the Confederacy 20,000 stands of arms taken from Federal arsenals. Alabama had furnished "full 27,000 of her men" to the Confederate army and "of these troops Alabama had armed more than 14,000."[46]

Louisiana's governor claimed to have borrowed $670,000 to arm the 20,202 men mustered into Confederate service from the state army.[47] Isham Harris of Tennessee organized, armed, and equipped twenty-one regiments of infantry, ten artillery companies, and almost a full regiment of cavalry in addition to regiments in Virginia and Pensacola. The armed, provisional force of Tennessee was transferred to the Confederate States on July 31, 1861.[48] Governor Brown of Georgia refused to allow arms belonging to the state to be carried out of Georgia by independent companies. But even he continued throughout his quarrels with the Confederate administration to arm regiments sent out by the state under requisition through the governor.[49]

While the states were exerting effort to send their requisitioned forces to the Confederate army properly armed, they also assumed another responsibility normally belonging to a central government—that of furnishing some of the clothing for the troops. In August, 1861, the Confederate congress provided money payments to state governors for clothing supplied to troops in the Confederate service.[50] State governments followed up this legislation with contracts to furnish uniforms and shoes to their respective armies serving the Confederacy.[51] According to Jonathan Worth, the North Carolina state clothing department grew to a "gigantic establishment."[52]

Other states were generous in their appropriations for soldiers' clothing. The South Carolina legislature set aside $171,000 for the purchase of shoes in 1863. Alabama arranged for the manufacture or purchase of 50,000 pairs of shoes in 1862. The Mississippi legislature negotiated for hides of beef slaughtered in the state to be used in making shoes for Mississippi soldiers.[53] In 1863 Georgia appropriated

$2,500,000 for shoes, clothing, caps, and hats for privates and non-commissioned officers. This amount rose in 1865 to $3,000,000 for subsistence, clothing, transportation, and medical supplies for Georgia soldiers. Although the efforts of state governments to continue aid to troops in the Confederate armies became a severe drain on state finances and definitely lightened the burdens of the central government, the states were never wholly successful in meeting the needs of their soldiers.

Subsistence for the Confederate armies proved to be as acute a problem as man-power, materiel, and clothing. To meet the need for food for its soldiers the Confederacy resorted early in the war to impressment, which, like conscription, was generally, if not unanimously, recognized as a necessary evil. Objections raised by legislatures and governors to Confederate impressment of foodstuff were concerned more with inequities in the operation of the system than with impressment *per se*. In response to pressure from states' sources, the war department warned its officers against seizing property belonging to the states. The Confederate secretary of war stated on August 6, 1862: "Necessity alone can warrant the impressment of private property for public use; and wherever the requisite supplies can be obtained by the consent of the owners at fair rates, and without hazardous delay, the military authorities will abstain from the harsh proceeding of impressment."[54]

Alleged abuses of the impressment policy, however, led to action on the part of state governments. The North Carolina legislature requested the governor to order the general in command in eastern North Carolina to equalize impressments so that no one person would suffer loss of all teams and wagons.[55] The Virginia general assembly asked Virginia congressman to seek means to make impressment more equitable.[56] The Confederate Congress responded to suggestions with attempts to improve impressment practice in the interests of the public. It passed an act allowing appraisement by disinterested parties when conflicting opinions arose over prices of impressed commodities. It exempted property necessary "for the support of the owner and his family, and to carry on the ordinary agricultural and mechanical business."[57] Apparently the reforms did little to ameliorate the harshness of impressment since public protests increased after their adoption. Laws in Alabama, Florida, Georgia, Louisiana, Mississippi, North Carolina, and Texas set up penalties for fraudulent seizures.[58] The South Carolina legislature requested further change in practice so as to insure just administration of the law.[59] The Georgia general assembly suggested that the secretary of war might well revoke appointment of impressment officers who were eligible for conscription and to place in their stead local impressment officials who were exempt from military service.[60]

The Confederate impressment law of 1863 set up commissions to determine just prices; and the procedure led to criticism of established price schedules. Southern newspapers did not always agree with opposition to impressment practices evinced in some quarters in their states. The Florida *Sentinel* questioned whether the system had, in fact, been abused.[61] The Houston *Telegraph*, the Galveston *News*, and the Texas *State Gazette* considered state acts interfering with impressment to be unwarranted meddling with the only means of supplying troops in the Trans-Mississippi Department.[62]

Impressment agents, however, sometimes unquestionably left much to be desired in their implementation of Confederate law. Letters from Governor John Milton to the secretary of war revealed that milch cows and calves were forcibly taken by commissary agents. It was the opinion of Milton that this practice along with the current scarcity of grain was responsible for desertion among Florida troops.[63] A revision of impressment laws corrected some of the objectionable features of previous acts. Congress forbade the taking of sheep, milch cows, or other stock and defined the term "just compensation" as the usual market price at the time and place of impressment.[64]

Impressment of labor also caused strain in Confederate-state relations, although the practice seemed in theory acceptable to state governors and legislatures. Here, too, it was the operation and not the principle that engendered friction. Even the strong state rights governor, Joseph Brown, accepted the fact that: "Negroes . . . may be taken by the Government for public use, on payment of just compensation."[65] The Confederate government, recognizing the complications that might arise in the process of commandeering Negro labor for defense works, was careful to work through state governors when possible in requisitioning labor. The impressment act of 1863 called for impressment of labor according to the laws of the states, where laws existed covering impressment.[66]

In the meantime requisitions for labor for Confederate defense works elicited reaction in the states. The South Carolina Executive Council tried to equalize the burden formerly resting on threatened areas in the state. It divided that portion of South Carolina which had not furnished slaves for defense into four districts. From each of those districts one-third of the laborers subject to road duty were to be drawn in successive months.[67] A law of December, 1862, set up a similar schedule enabling the governor to apportion quotas among the owners in such district in turn.[68] The secretary of war was unable to accept several sections of the South Carolina act for want of congressional authorization; and for a time the governor proceeded under the Council system.[69] Upon a later threat of an extension of Confederate impressment of labor, the South Carolina legislature enacted a law designed to be more effective and at the same time acceptable to the central government, although it, too, embodied some restrictions upon the use of impressed labor.[70] The advance of General William T. Sherman prevented the testing of the new law. But until the end of the war planters continued to complain that the system was "tyrannical unjust & should be expunged."[71]

When the Virginia governor received orders in 1862 to impress labor for the Confederacy, his legislature passed an implementing act.[72] The success of the Virginia law depended largely on the county courts which administered it. In some counties dilatory tactics brought delay in meeting slave requisitions; and in other counties nothing at all was accomplished.[73] Opponents of impressment of labor used as propaganda a remark allegedly made by General Robert E. Lee to the effect that Negroes should be left on the farms.[74] In time, pressure by the planters brought results and in 1864 the legislature, by resolution, asked the governor to confer with Confederate authorities in an effort to secure release of Negroes from the latest requisition.[75]

Leaders in other states seemed dissatisfied with the demands of the Confederacy for Negro labor and at one time or another sought to retain control over slave impressment. The Florida legislature was exceptionally defiant in passing a law in 1864 which stated that "No demand as impressment of slaves . . . shall be made, except in conformity with the provisions of this law; and if any shall be made in violation thereof, it is hereby declared unlawful and void."[76]

It appears that state legislation controlling slave impressment was designed to obtain for Negroes better working conditions and adequate compensation to owners along with an equitable distribution of the burden among slave-owners. Nevertheless, opposition to impressment of their slaves was so intense among planters that even the best efforts of state governors and legislatures were of little avail.

Although no historians of the Confederacy can ignore the clashes between the Confederacy and the states on matters involving man-power, materiel of war and supply for the Confederate armies, none should neglect the areas of Confederate-state harmony which existed. And nowhere was state support for Confederate policies more consistent than in Confederate finance. In 1861 Louisiana confiscated and turned over to the Confederacy $389,267 found in the New Orleans mint and customshouse.[77] This, with a $500,000 loan offered by Alabama, made up the purse with which the Confederacy began operations.[78] When the Confederacy levied a direct tax in 1861, the states, with the exception of Mississippi and Texas, assumed the tax.[79]

Southern states strove in many ways to encourage sale of Confederate bonds and to promote faith in Confederate treasury notes. The Alabama legislature continued suspension of specie payments by chartered banks on condition that

they receive at par Confederate notes for debts due them.[80]
In Virginia, banks could lend to state and Confederacy thirty
per cent of their capital, in proportionate ratio of twenty
per cent to the state and ten per cent to the central government. The law specified that "A loan to either shall impose
an obligation of loan to the other." Local units of government in the states were directed to appoint commissioners
to collect subscriptions for Confederate bonds.[81]

Legislation in a number of instances approved the use of
Confederate notes to fulfill obligations to the states. Some
legislatures went further and tried by law or resolution to
encourage acceptance of Confederate currency for private
debts. More cooperation with Confederate financial policies
was forthcoming in 1862 when Secretary of the Treasury
C. G. Memminger suggested that Southern states might
bolster Confederate credit by guaranteeing the payment of
the national debt. Alabama, Florida, Mississippi, and South
Carolina legislatures complied by endorsing the Confederate
debt in proportion to their respective representation in congress or in some similar fashion.[82] Texas accepted responsibility in an unusual manner. The legislature there declared
that "Should the State of Texas . . . withdraw from her
association as a member of the Confederate States before the
indebtedness of the said Confederacy is fully paid, the faith
of the State will be pledged to the payment of her prorata
portion of such remaining indebtedness."[83]

When the proposal came before the Georgia general
assembly, Governor Brown announced his disapproval. His
reason was that compliance would strengthen the central
government at the expense of the states. The Savannah
Daily Morning News upheld the governor's opposition.[84] The
consensus in Georgia seemed to be that state credit must be
kept unimpaired to afford a home currency if depreciation
of Confederate treasury notes continued. Like Georgia,
North Carolina failed to support the guarantee measure,
giving to state rights arguments a different slant from those
of Georgia. Since the Confederate government was the agent
of the states, the argument went, states were automatically

bound to the extent of their share of the debt of the Confederacy without any implementing state legislation.[85]

In summary, it seems obvious that, despite the "disorganizing instincts" in Southern states, the Confederacy would have gotten off to a slow start in 1861 had governors, legislatures, and conventions failed to support Confederate policies and programs. Southern states gave of their money, their men, and their supplies with a generosity tempered only by estimates of local security. The increase in tension between Confederate and state authorities over conscription and impressment laws was due generally to presumed abuses in the framework and implementation of the laws rather than to the principle behind the measures. And despite tension and quarrels, states legislatures and most of the state governors continued day by day support for the Confederacy's financial policies. As for the suspension of the writ of habeas corpus and use of martial law, prevailing opinion in the South held the suspension law unconstitutional and the practice dangerous. It is not surprising that Southerners resisted with interposition of state law this alleged violation of the Confederate constitution.

During the last months of war, demoralization of state governments and breakdown of state finances became general throughout the South. These conditions coupled with despondency over military defeats led the legislatures and governors of several states to make gestures of further cooperation with Confederate military measures. In May, 1864, for example, Texas turned over to Confederate service the state troops she had earlier retained, upon receiving assurance that frontier defense would not be disturbed.[86] Later, Mississippi's governor relinquished to the Confederacy the remnants of his state army.[87] In 1864 Governor Vance of North Carolina wrote to governors of Mississippi, South Carolina, Georgia, Alabama, Florida, Tennessee, and Virginia requesting a meeting to work out some plan: "Beyond all else, men must be sent to the armies of Generals Lee and Hood," he said.[88] At the conference held at Vance's instigation, the governors resolved to use their "best exertions to increase the effective forces of our armies."[89] The Florida legislature in revising its militia laws gave Confederate commanders authority to order militia out for duty when a call upon the governor was impossible.[90] The Georgia legislation providing for a *levy en masse* directed the governor to confer with Confederate authorities "So that the whole physical force which both governments can bring to the field may be employed alike and in common, for the defense of State and Confederate independence."[91]

The "whole physical force" of the Confederacy and the states was not, of course, mobilized. And, in the light of the deteriorating economy and dwindling morale in Southern states by 1864, it is highly unlikely that it could have been mustered or maintained.

★

IV

ECONOMIC LEGISLATION

LINCOLN'S ELECTION and the separatist agitation of 1860-1861 disrupted normal commercial transactions in the South. The economic instability which set in depressed the public confidence so necessary to a healthy economy. Normality never returned; and for most Southern people economic needs grew increasingly more difficult to fulfill.

There were business enterprises that flourished despite the abnormal conditions. Banks, first to feel the rigors of uncertainty, soon recovered and even expanded operations. In part recovery was due to the efforts of state legislatures to adjust banking laws to the unusual circumstances which war and invasion created and in part to the speculative opportunities inherent in war times.

As early as November, 1860, Georgia, South Carolina, and North Carolina legislatures and conventions allowed banks to suspend specie payments.[1] Texas and Arkansas had no banks; but in 1861 other state legislatures or executives authorized suspension of specie payment.[2] When suspension resulted in hoarding of privately held gold and silver, legislatures or conventions began to relax restrictions on bank note issues. Tennessee laws permitted the Bank of Tennessee to circulate notes of any denominations "not less than the sum of one dollar" and later in 1861 "of less than $1 on the same terms and conditions that said bank is now authorized to issue notes of larger denominations."[3] Other states enacted similar measures.

Mississippi, Georgia, and South Carolina tried speculative banking schemes to aid the farmer.[4] Mississippi's legislators chartered a bank capitalized at $1,000,000, with cotton at $25 per bale acceptable for subscription notes. Subscribers were to hold cotton until the blockade was raised, at which time they could sell it for specie with which to pay off cotton notes.[5] Georgia established such a bank at Thomasville, in which the capital stock was $3,000,000 paid for in cotton at $30 a bale or in state or Confederate bonds.[6] The South Carolina general assembly authorized creation of one branch bank in each of the state's congressional districts to issue stock on cotton notes, $6 for every hundred pounds of short staple and $15 for every hundred pounds of long staple cotton.[7]

John Christopher Schwab, a historian of Confederate finance, concluded that such prosperity as Southern banks enjoyed came through their war-time speculations rather than through the usual avenues of banking activities.[8] State legislatures did try to curb speculative or wildcat banking, but not always successfully. For example, charters granted in Alabama, Tennessee, and North Carolina, during war years, sometimes specified that new banking corporations must receive a portion of their capital stock in gold or silver before they could begin operations.[9] An act in Virginia forbade payment of dividends at rates higher than six per cent until banks should have accumulated a contingent fund amounting to at least five per cent of its capital stock. Florida banks were "strictly enjoined and required to present regular quarterly reports of their conditions to the governor."[10] The regulations were apparently not too binding, for regular banking interests did well during the war. Schwab states, "We hear of none winding up their affairs, and, on the other hand, we find dividends paid with great regularity on bank stock until the close of hostilities, or . . . as long as we have any records of the Southern money market, namely, till January, 1865."[11]

While bankers found currency of one kind or another to keep them in business, farmers suffered severely. Laws could do little in invaded areas to prevent the demoralization of labor, contraction of market, disruption of transportation lines, and destruction of equipment. Even farm lands remote from the sound of guns felt the effects of the blockade, inadequacy of railroad facilities, and manpower shortage. Early in the war, moreover, there appeared three agricultural problems of great severity: the over-production of cotton, the under-production of foodstuff, and the scarcity of salt; and these problems state governments did endeavor to relieve.

Confederate reliance upon cotton as a diplomatic weapon did not win unanimous acceptance among Southerners. Even so, Southern leaders generally acknowledged the need for converting to grain some of the acreage devoted to cotton. Governor John Pettus of Mississippi recommended to his legislature that some measure be adopted to prevent the accumulation of several crops of cotton during the blockade. He suggested "onerous taxes" on cotton.[12] The Mississippi general assembly would go no further at the time than to appeal for cotton curtailment on a voluntary basis and to require counties to submit statistical information on crop acreages. In 1863 the legislature levied a tax of five cents on each pound of seed cotton produced in excess of one 500-pound bale of ginned cotton per laborer.[13]

Arguments in favor of restricting cotton production came from people in all walks of life. A small farmer wrote to the governor of Alabama:

> There is an other thing that has distressed me a great deal and that is the next cotton crop. I have traveled through this section a good deal and I find the people are aiming to plant near a full crop of cotton if wee [sic] don't have some more reverses. . . . My impression is that won [sic] amongst the best laws that congress could have passed would have been a law confiscating all the cotton . . . and as congress has not done it if our state could do something towards stopping of it my impreshion [sic] is it would be a good thing . . . it appears to me wee are thinking more of the cotton and dollar than of our country.[14]

The Alabama law on cotton planting levied a tax of ten cents per pound on seed cotton over and above 2500 pounds to each hand employed in its production, each pound of ginned cotton to be estimated as equal to four pounds of seed cotton.[15]

Arkansas limited production of cotton to two acres for

each hand and set up stiff penalties for violations.[16] The
Florida law was more stringent, limiting planting to one
acre for each hand between the ages of fifteen and sixty and
one acre to each two hands above or below the ages specified.
Plantation owners could plant one-fourth of an acre in
tobacco per laborer. Exemption from the provisions of the
law favored those who manufactured their cotton into cloth
for family use or for sale at prices below those set by state
commissioners. The Florida *Sentinel* in commenting on the
law urged compliance with it regardless of doubtful constitutionality, on the grounds of its necessity.[17]

Governor Brown of Georgia supported legislation limiting
cotton production. He wrote to Linton Stephens that over-
production of cotton was more to be feared than any other
"disadvantage under which we labor."[18] A Georgia planter
reported to the governor that, in his opinion, nine-tenths of
the cotton planters approved regulation.[19] The Georgia law
allowing three acres for each hand was weaker than that of
Alabama, Arkansas, or Florida.[20] Brown asked for a reduction to one-fourth acre per hand; but the legislature
was unwilling to restrict production to this extent.[21]
Although several states refrained from regulating cotton
production, much land within their boundaries was volun-
tarily diverted from this staple to food crops.[22]

But cotton remained the basic Southern crop; and producers suffered first from the embargo policy of the Confederacy and later from the blockade. Louisiana lawmakers
were amenable to measures relieving the distress of planters
left without a market for their crops and without cash for
taxes and other expenses. The legislature passed a relief bill
providing for treasury notes secured by pledges of the cotton
crop of 1861.[23] The New Orleans *Daily Crescent* warned
against such an inflationary measure and the Natchitoches
Union commended the governor for his veto of the bill.[24] A
letter to the governor indicated that news of the veto had
"produced great rejoicing in this community, where I do not
suppose there is a single man of any responsibility that could
be found in favour of such a measure."[25] Mississippi put into

effect a law similar to that vetoed in Louisiana, making $5,000,000 available to planters who would hold cotton in security for notes issued at the rate of five cents a pound.[26]

State legislatures also sought to increase the supply of food by prohibiting distillation of grain and other products into whiskey. Indeed, few of the general laws relative to the production of whiskey passed by Southern legislatures were inspired by concern for morals or law and order; rather, the objective seems to have been conservation of foodstuff for soldiers and for home consumption.[27] In December, 1861, a North Carolinian wrote to one of the convention delegates complaining that eleven stills within a radius of eleven miles had bought up almost all the corn at "near $4 per bushel." This writer disapproved of taxing the stills since the consumer would ultimately pay the tax.[28] The North Carolina convention, however, employed both the tax method of control and prohibition, levying a tax of thirty cents a gallon on whiskey made before April 16, 1862, and prohibiting distillation of corn, wheat, rye, oats, of mixtures of grains after that date. It imposed a tax of one dollar on every gallon of whiskey brought into the state before March 1, 1862.[29]

When the legislature of North Carolina met in the fall of 1862, it prohibited distillation of whiskey from a variety of agricultural products. The state's distillers must have exercised ingenuity in evading the purposes of the law, since amendatory legislation increased the number of proscribed products and specified that the law cover beer or any other malt liquor.[31] Arkansas laws forbade production of liquor from grain, potatoes, sugar, molasses, or syrups.[32]

In 1862 Florida had prohibited distillation of grain into whiskey, except under government contract. The law evidently was ineffective since by the fall of 1863 General P. G. T. Beauregard was asking the governor to sponsor a measure which would conserve sugar and molasses by preventing the use of these products for rum.[33] Governor Milton's address to the legislature pointed up the necessity for immediate action.[34] A new law gave the governor the right to abate as a nuisance any distillery existing contrary to provisions of the act and revoked all previously granted licenses.[35]

Governor Shorter of Alabama closed distilleries in his state in 1862 without authority from the legislature and appealed to that body to support his action. The legislature in response placed distillation of grain under the control of the state. The governor was to "prescribe regulations . . . to appoint agents, make contracts . . . to cause the liquors to be disposed of as he might see fit." Net profits would go for relief of indigent families of Alabama soldiers in the Confederate service.[36] The law was difficult to enforce; and later the general assembly ordered the governor to send a list of licensed distilleries to the commandants of home reserves, who were responsible for preventing unauthorized production of whiskey.[37] One approving reaction was registered by a Mobile laborer who wrote to his wife: "I saw old Titus here again yesterday, but I dont think he will stay here long as there is no more whiskay [*sic*] to be had in Mobile. i think the Confederate State have joined the Temperance Society, & it has done a gret [*sic*] deal of good."[38] In 1864, revised legislation left the licensing of Alabama distillers in the hands of county commissioners.[39] South Carolina, like Alabama, restricted distillation in 1862 and created a state monopoly of whiskey administered by district agents.

At Governor Brown's request, the Georgia legislature passed a law which, like that of North Carolina, prohibited unlicensed distillation of spirituous liquors from a great variety of products and ordered the governor to issue the licenses that were necessary.[40] Mississippi followed the action of other states by conserving corn, rye, sugar, and molasses.[41] In 1864, licensing was authorized for two distilleries to produce whiskey for medicinal purposes, and distribution of the "medicinal product" was placed in the hands of state and county agents.[42] In March of 1865, The Harris County *Enterprise* reported that General Nathan Bedford Forrest had been counseling the legislators on anti-distillation measures. It was alleged that he said: "Gentlemen, you may pass what laws you please about distillation, but as sure as my name is Bedford Forrest, I'll break up every distillery, unauthorized or authorized, that I can find, and hang every —————— that runs one."[43]

When the Louisiana legislature enacted prohibition, it imposed serious penalties for violation, the offense carrying a maximum fine of $15,000 and maximum imprisonment of twelve months.[44] Virginia experimented for a time with different measures and finally prohibited whiskey production from grains, fruit, potatoes, sugar, and other canes. Opposition to the law found expression in the Richmond *Whig*, which compared the 1862 measure to the fanaticism of abolitionism, calling it a "gross repudiation of the obligations of contracts . . . but the substantial effect of the modern law is to take the property of private individuals and give it, at cheap rates, to the multitude. This is the first step toward agrarianism."[46]

Texas came tardily to accept the necessity of limiting the supply of whiskey and thereby increasing that of foodstuff. County courts were empowered to declare distilleries "prejudicial to public subsistence."[47] The *State Gazette* believed that the law would bring distillation to a stop altogether.[48]

Southern states which regulated cotton and grain production were even more alert to balance the supply of salt with consumer needs. Ella Lonn in her intensive study of the salt problem in the Confederacy said: "The fact that salt could become a major problem to the Confederacy reveals the industrial backwardness of the South, its complete dependence on outside sources for primary needs and emphasizes that fact as the most serious of its disadvantages in the unequal struggle."[49]

Having an ample supply from Avery Island and Lake Bisteneau, Louisiana was one state in which the salt problem became solely one of transportation and control of speculation.[50] Even there public lands containing salt springs or saline waters were withdrawn from sale at the land offices.[51] In other states laws and ordinances gave to state agencies partial or complete control over the supply and distribution of this necessitous commodity.

The North Carolina convention established a salt commissioner who could purchase or lease land for salt works to manufacture and furnish salt at cost to the people of each county.[52] North Carolina salt works in Virginia supplemented private production.[53] A North Carolina law permitted county justices of the peace to make appropriations from tax revenue to maintain an adequate supply on hand.[54] Jonathan Worth, the state salt commissioner, was dissatisfied with the work of his agents and issued orders that salt should be paid for before delivery to the counties. He believed that the commission should be returning money into the state treasury rather than receiving doles from that source.[55] State aid continued, however, throughout the war. In addition to financial aid, the North Carolina legislature tried to save labor for work in salt production by relieving operatives from militia duty and by requesting their exemption from conscription.[56]

Governor A. B. Moore of Alabama had authority to take possession of all salt stored or held for sale. A jury of twelve freeholders or householders could assess the price if disagreement occurred between governor and owner. The legislature further directed the governor to lease salt springs or wells belonging to the state provided that lessees would agree to sell at a price fixed by the state.[57] One legislator who approved the policy of the general assembly wrote that, according to rumor, enough salt was held in Montgomery and Mobile to take care of the entire state.[58] But as might be expected, Alabama critics condemned the operation of the state salt works and the principle of direct action on the part of the state in this business enterprise.[59]

A somewhat favorable report of the state's efforts to supply salt appeared in the Montgomery *Mail* in late 1862 in an announcement that the salt works were turning out from 500 to 600 bushels a day and that "their capacity for production is daily augmenting."[60] In 1863 the salt commissioner of Alabama was bartering salt for labor and supplies, giving about one bushel of salt for eight bushels of corn and peas, 500 pounds of fodder, or eighteen pounds of bacon. After a year's operation the state had spent $1,000,000, had paid for labor and supplies, and had turned over to the quartermaster 20,000 bushels at $8 per bushel.[61]

Georgia and South Carolina attacked the salt shortage first by subsidies. In 1861 the Georgia general assembly offered $50,000 as a loan without interest to any company manufacturing salt. The legislature appropriated an additional $500,000 at the next annual session for the "purchase or manufacture and transportation of salt on State account, or in giving encouragement and substantial aid to any responsible individual or association who may be engaged . . . in the purchase or manufacture of salt for distribution without speculation." The governor received legislative approval for his expenditures of money and labor in Virginia at salt works on contracts for the state.[62] Governor Brown wrote to Colonel John Harris that the state works at Saltville were producing 500 bushels per day; the Troup Company, 600; and the Augusta Company, 300 bushels per day in 1862. He felt that the necessary balance was in the hands of speculators and hoped for authority to "open the dark places where the salt is hid."[63] The next year the legislature made an effort to prevent private monopoly of coast lands adapted to salt production.[64]

Mississippians were beginning to feel a pinch of salt shortage in 1862. A contemporary diary records that no salt was for sale in Jackson and Vicksburg in October of that year; but that the governor was sending two steamers to Louisiana for an adequate amount.[65] An ample supply for state needs had not been consistently maintained in 1863; and the legislature, therefore, set aside $500,000 for salt works. Under this law Mississippi purchased several hundred acres of timber land in Alabama and put several salt wells with necessary appurtenances into operation.[66]

Texas had the good fortune to obtain a salt lake which had been in litigation for some time. To supplement the salt works there, the legislature ordered the military board to investigate salines on the Northwestern frontier of the state and appropriated money for the purpose.[67]

The Virginia legislature was slow to interpose its authority over privately owned saline works. Contracts were made with salt companies in an effort to meet the needs of the people; and county courts were directed to purchase and distribute salt for their localities.[68] Nothing more was done until September, 1862, when a special session of the general assembly convened to consider the salt problem. An act passed then gave the governor the right to seize property, real or personal, for salt production if he should deem it necessary. The law made it mandatory to fill the needs of Virginia before meeting contracts with other states.[69] The governor, after an inspection trip to the salt works, decided to postpone appropriation of the works.[70] Later the situation became so unsatisfactory that Virginia established a salt superintendency for production of this commodity. The Richmond *Sentinel* suggested that the state apply the same sort of action to the acquisition of other scarce consumer products.[71]

In all states consumer products were growing scarce. Bread and salt were necessities on the home front, true; but so were shoes, textiles, implements, medicines, and countless other articles needed as urgently by civilians as by soldiers. As states had grappled with the shortages of grain and salt, so they endeavored to meet other demands.

Political leadership and public opinion looked first to private enterprise to fill the production gaps. As the Washington *Telegraph* put it:

Workshops, and spinning mills, and forges, and cabinet shops, and paper mills cannot of course be created by the Legislature. The State cannot spend its money or lend its credit that way . . . But legislation can do much to encourage private enterprise and remove obstacles.[72]

The Arkansas legislature was rather conservative in its lending of state credit. It appropriated $300,000 to be used as funds for persons willing to engage in the manufacture of salt, iron, or cotton cards and up to 160 acres of land as an inducement.[73] Several states were more liberal with subsidies, bonuses, and other aid. Alabama offered a bonus of ten cents, eight cents, and six cents per pair on cotton and wool cards of various makes.[74] Mississippi's bonus for cotton and wool cards in 1863 reached $5 per pair.[75] The governor of Virginia received permission to aid in the productivity of mines by hiring or impressing labor and to permit persons manufacturing saltpetre to take wood, earth, and other material off public lands.[76] Mississippi allowed tanyard operators to cut oaktree bark from state land.[77] Texas offered a land grant of 320 acres for every $1,000 invested in machinery to produce iron, cotton or woolen cloth, firearms, nitre, sulphur, powder, salt, cotton, or woolen cards, spinning jennies, paper, or oil.[78] North Carolina laws established loans up to $10,000 to persons manufacturing cotton and woolen cards to sell to citizens of the state.[79]

Despite the generosity of legislatures and the great number of companies chartered during the war, private production failed to keep abreast of demand for manufactured goods. The Richmond *Enquirer* bemoaned the fact that monied men hesitated to venture into manufacturing, preferring rather to buy or foreclose on real property or to run the blockade.[80] In the emergency the states took the logical step of entering into direct trade and manufacture and succeeded remarkably well under the circumstances.

Alabama allocated $60,000 in 1862 for purchase of cotton and woolen cards "beyond the limits of this State" to be sold for cost to the white population. The state also contracted with local companies for cards.[81]

Virginia created a state agency in Richmond to buy and sell raw cotton, cotton yarns, cotton cloth, cotton and woolen cards. By the same law it permitted requisitions upon cotton factories in the state for yarn and cloth.[82] Florida entered into a contract with the Florida Card Manufacturing Company to purchase 2500 pairs of cotton and 500 pairs of woolen cards.[83] The Florida *Sentinel* complimented the governor on the price of $6.00 per pair; these articles brought in some places $20 to $25 a pair.[84] The military board in Texas secured a supply of cards; but from contemporary correspondence it appears that the distribution of the cards was inefficiently and inequitably handled.[85] In North Carolina the General assembly directed its governor to purchase

250,000 cotton cards and 50,000 woolen cards through its agent in Europe in 1863.[86]

The activities of state legislatures and governors led them far away from the normal scope of peace-time legislation. Virginia, Georgia, North Carolina, Louisiana, Texas, and South Carolina were most aggressive in their trading and manufacturing enterprise. The first objective of the states in sending agents to Europe and elsewhere had been that of obtaining war materiel. When consumer shortages grew more acute, contracts came to include a variety of good on state accounts; and state direct trading activities grew more involved.

Georgia had dispatched T. Butler King to Europe in 1861 and later sent C. G. Baylor over. The governor entrusted Solomon Leopold Waitzfelder with the responsibility of purchasing cotton in Georgia for the state, card wire in Europe for state manufacturing and in 1865 authorized this agent to sell Georgia goods in Nassau, Bermuda, and other depositories "at best advantage for state."[87]

North Carolina sent John White as its first commissioner to Europe; and White negotiated for loans of money to be discharged in cotton deliverable after the war.[88] The state authorized the governor to unite with Alexander Collie & Company in the purchase of one-fourth interest in four steamers to be employed in import-export trade with Europe or the West Indies;[89] and the legislature approved the governor's purchase of the *Advance* for the same purpose.[90] The state program for foreign purchases suffered somewhat from a conflict arising between two agents, Duncan McRae and George N. Sanders, both of whom had received appointments from the governor. J. S. Amis wrote Vance that the friction over authority existing between the two men had caused some little impatience on the part of the legislature toward the state's operations. He feared that a strong disposition to withhold money might result and suggested holding subordinates to rigid and regular exhibits of accounts.[91]

The South Carolina legislature provided for a "union of the State with the Importing and Exporting Company of South Carolina." The law authorized the state to become one-fourth owner of the ships of the company and to export cotton and other produce to pay for imported supplies for soldiers and citizens alike.[92]

State governments did not depend wholly on trade to obtain goods. Several expanded penitentiary production for wartime demands. Some idea of the diversification of activity in the penitentiaries can be seen from a description of losses sustained when General Ulysses S. Grant burned the Mississippi penitentiary. The Mississippi Senate Journal listed the following items as a loss: a cotton factory, "2,304 spindles, 76 osnaburg looms and 4 twill loom . . . 7 sets of carpenters and cabinet tools, 1 set of cooper tools, two wood lathes, 1 large iron lathe, one gear-cutting machine, one sixty-horse power engine and three boilers . . . shoe and tailor's shop . . . cotton shed containing 300 bales of cotton. . . ."[93]

The Georgia general assembly commissioned the state's master armorer to examine the machinery of John Lee & Company, manufacturers of cotton and woolen cards, with a view toward purchasing cards or buying the factory or an interest in it.[94] The state entered into an agreement with Divine, Jones, and Lee Company in December of 1862 for one-half interest in the business, the operations of which were carried on within the state penitentiary.[95]

John Milton, governor of Florida, sent an emissary to Georgia to observe the machines for making cards in the hope that Florida might imitate Georgia's initiative.[96] When Governor Lubbock of Texas wrote Brown for information about the operations, he stated that Texas had but one cloth manufactory, that of the state penitentiary, and there existed a "desperate need for some other source."[97] Governor Brown's experiment caught the attention of North Carolina's chief executive as well. The legislature of that state directed the governor to negotiate for the purchase of a card-manufacturing machine from Georgia. Brown was unable to accommodate North Carolina to that extent; but he did outline his plan to Governor Vance and suggested that Vance might send a machinist to Georgia to duplicate the operations.[98]

One of the most enterprising of the state governors was

Louisiana's Henry Watkins Allen. Numbered among Louisiana's achievements during his administration were a cloth factory, turpentine stills, and an iron foundry.[99] Allen reported in 1865 that the state had a castor oil plant, a baking soda factory, distilleries for medicinal alcohol, and laboratories for indigenous medicines.[100]

Distribution of state-owned commodities followed different patterns in different states. The Georgia legislature gave the governor power to make arrangements for sale of state-manufactured articles.[101] Often goods were sold by public auction.[102] County officials or appointed local agents in some states handled the distribution of products usually for cost, sometimes free. In Virginia the legislature permitted county or city courts to choose storekeepers selected from those exempt from conscription to sell or distribute articles to consumers.[103] Louisiana's governor made use of the state store system where state goods could be purchased for depreciated Louisiana currency.[104]

The efforts of governors and legislators at trade and manufacturing, direct or regulatory, were somewhat frustrated by transportation bottlenecks. Although Southern railway mileage had reached a respectable figure of about 8,783 miles in 1861, the lines were largely a "nondescript sequence of separate roads."[105] Continuity of traffic suffered from interruptions due to gaps between lines, differences in track gauge, or failure of lines to join tracks at junction points. Such service as did exist was a result of the credit backing given by state governments, county governments, and municipalities.

The story of Southern railroads during the Civil War, so admirably told by Robert C. Black, is tragic. The gloss of paper profits could not conceal attrition of track, locomotives, rolling stock, and destruction of material by Federal and Confederate troops. The Confederate government came slowly to the position long since occupied by states and began to aid and supervise transportation lines. Meanwhile states continued that paternalism—aid in the form of money and land—which had greatly affected the development of transportation in the old South.

Tennessee's largess to railroads before the war had reached the figure of $17,000,000. The legislature amended the code relating to railway loans in May, 1861, to give the governor discretionary rather than mandatory power to appoint recievers for lines defaulting in payment of interest on state loans.[106]

North Carolina track approximated 900 miles in 1861. According to one authority, the state during the war gave aid to every railroad except one either in the form of stock subscriptions or loans.[107] South Carolina pledged her credit in guaranteeing railroad bonds and made outright gifts of money and land.[108] A report from the comptroller-general's office in 1863, stated that South Carolina had aided all of the twelve railroads operating in the state at some time during the year.[109]

Although an Alabama correspondent for the Montgomery *Mail* pointed out that the state had no rail connections to all points on her border, he added optimistically, "But, thank God, it is in the power of her Legislature to apply the remedy."[110] The law makers sought to apply the remedy. They appropriated special funds for the purchase of stock in the Alabama and Tennessee River Railroad Company and lent to the Alabama and Florida Railroad the sum of $30,000. They gave the $40,000, earlier ear-marked for the Selma and Gulf Railroad, to the Alabama and Mississippi River Railroad in an effort to expedite the completion of the line from Selma to Meridian, Mississippi.[111]

Georgia, at the outbreak of the war, possessed in her own right one state line and had within her boundaries seven other major railroad companies. And before 1861 had passed, the state seized the Brunswick and Florida Railroad. This action followed the unwillingness of Northern stockholders to maintain the line, which was of considerable military importance to Georgia.[112]

Arkansas aided the Memphis and Little Rock Railroad Company with stock subscriptions and loans.[113] Louisiana authorized the payment of bonds in the amount of $6,000 per mile of road graded to the Vicksburg, Shreveport, and Texas Railroad Company; the Baton Rouge, Gross Tete, and Opelousas Railroad Company; the Central Stem of the Mississippi and Pacific Railroad Company; and the New Orleans, Opelousas, and Great Western Railroad Company.[114]

Governor Letcher's message to the Virginia legislature in December, 1861, pointed out the necessity of completing several links in the railroad system of the state.[115] The legislature permitted the Richmond, Fredericksburg, and Potomac Railroad to increase its stock in order to effect a junction with the Orange and Alexandria and the Manassas Gap Railroads. It also empowered the board of public works to construct a road for military purposes connecting the Manassas Gap Railroad with the Winchester and Potomac Railroad.[116] In October of 1862, the Virginia general assembly determined to devote the available resources of the commonwealth to the construction of railroads.[117]

State encouragement of railroad expansion took the familiar form of land grants as well as capital and credit advances. Louisiana, Florida, Mississippi, Alabama, and Texas were generous in this respect.[118] Texas also repeatedly granted extension of time for compliance with charter terms in her effort to protect railroad interests.[119] And a more questionable aspect of state aid to railroads appeared in this state and in Mississippi, where special interest groups worked for and obtained laws permitting the railroads to repay state loans in depreciated currency. In 1862 Texas railroads even wrested from the general assembly deferment of interest payment on loans made to railroads from the special school fund. Two years later, railroads which had received state bonds or treasury warrants at par could repay the state in the same currency.[120] The Mississippi law enabled railroads to repay loans in gold and silver or in the treasury notes of the state at par.[121]

The unsettled times led railroad companies occasionally to evade the normal liability of carriers for freight loss and damage. The Georgia legislature protected the public by holding railroads to full liability and by declaring null any contracts to the contrary.[122] Mississippi, Texas, and South Carolina enacted similar safeguards for consigners of freight and baggage.[123] Several states attempted to force carriers to promote the safety and comfort of passengers. Mississippi and Georgia conductors and agents had to keep a light burning through the nights in cars and stations and to have on hand a supply of water and fire when demanded by passengers.[124] The Florida legislature held railroad employees subject to indictment if guilty of negligence or carelessness resulting in injury.[125] Nevertheless, many accidents did occur. After a serious mishap in Alabama in 1864, the Alabama legislators enacted a rather amusing remedy for such collisions.

Whenever the tracks of separate and independent railroads cross each other, it shall be the duty of all engine drivers and conductors to cause the trains which they respectively drive and conduct, to come to a full stop within fifty feet of the place of crossing and then to move forward slowly—the train of the eldest road to have the privilege of crossing first.[126]

State governments ventured into rate-fixing as freight and passenger tariffs mounted during the war. Florida at first required free transportation for property or troops of state and central government.[127] This law was repealed within a year of its passage; and the Florida Board of Internal Improvements received the power to establish rates in 1864.[128] Alabama encouraged free transportation of military personnel and supplies by exempting from taxes companies which hauled troops and munitions without charge.[129] Louisiana and North Carolina legisaltors provided for committees to investigate certain railroad companies to determine whether unfair advantage had been taken of shippers.[130] The Virginia legislature set up a schedule of rates to which railroads had to adhere.[131] Pressure for repeal of this restriction, however, led to a change in the law, permitting the companies to appeal to the board of public works.[132]

The combined exertions of State governments, however, could not arrest deterioration of railroad equipment and service. Replacements of iron, spikes, rolling stock, and locomotives became impossible. Newspapers and other contemporary sources of information relate instances of rotting food accumulating in stations, food needed with equal despera-

tion by soldier and civilian. The breakdown of rail transportation had serious consequences on the home front as
well as on the battlefield.

In grappling with economic problems, state legislators and
governors showed courage and initiative. Courage was needed
to face resentment aroused by state control of agricultural
production. Initiative was required to launch state-owned
and state-operated trading and manufacturing establishments
at a time when managerial knowledge was limited in the
South and general conditions most disadvantageous. And
undoubtedly the overall effectiveness of the state programs
suffered from administrative difficulties. Not the least of the
administrative problems arose from the role of county officials as enforcement agents for regulation and as distribution agents for commodities. The system made for inefficiency
and favoritism. Deterioration of morale among civilians was
as pronounced in those states with active economic programs
as in those whose legislatures and governors hesitated to
undertake new or expanded economic activities.

★

V

INSTITUTIONAL STABILITY

DEFENSE MEASURES, Confederate relations, and economic problems ranked high on state legislative agenda. At the same time, governors and legislators recognized the importance of maintaining, insofar as possible, normal political and cultural conditions. Control of Negro labor, operation of courts, preservation of law and order, and continuation of civil government and of cultural institutions received major attention from state governments.

Southern labor was something more than a factor of production, for the presence of several million slaves had profoundly influenced the mores of the region. Slavery, under fire for decades, now faced threat of extinction by force of arms; and the outbreak of hostilities greatly intensified fear of Negro insurrection. The degree of anxiety varied with time and place; but letters and diaries of the period indicate that this dread hung like an ominous cloud over the Southern mind throughout the long conflict.

The outbreak of war brought a general tightening of slave codes. In 1861 Florida strengthened regulations governing patrols—white men who made the rounds of plantation areas to see that slave codes were enforced—by making the militia subject to patrol duty and requiring weekly rounds. Laws in other states empowered county courts or justices of the peace to appoint or organize patrol detachments. In most instances the revised codes required patrols to make their rounds more frequently, usually once a week, increased their authority, and subjected them to penalties for failure to perform prescribed duties.[1]

The Virginia legislature created a county police force to arrest persons suspected of inciting slaves to rebellion or escape; and in Tennessee "five credible persons" could bring before the court anyone suspected of insurrectionary activity. It became a capital offense to circulate incendiary activity among North Carolina slaves.[2]

State legislatures revamped measures relating to resident supervision of the farm Negroes. Some states refused to permit owners to place slaves over fellow laborers in units separated from the home place and required the presence of a white man wherever slaves were located.[3]

As runaway slaves grew more numerous during war, state legislatures enacted or amended laws in an effort to facilitate capture and return of the fugitives. Georgia's law of 1865, providing for the stationing of mounted pickets at strategic points to apprehend runaways, indicates the seriousness of the problem.[4]

An increasing preoccupation with laws relating to crime and punishment further showed concern over lawlessness among the Negroes. Such measures took a variety of forms such as were found in old slave codes, but there was a tendency to increase punishment for crimes of arson, larceny, and burglary by slaves and other offenses and to regulate more carefully the sale of whiskey to Negroes. Surprisingly little attention was given to miscegenation. The citizens of Barnwell district in South Carolina petitioned their legislators to take action against white men who were consorting with Negro and mulatto women "in a manner disreputable to the neighborhoods in which they reside, setting a pernicious example to our youth and assailing the institution of slavery through the process of a tolerated amalgamation." The Committee on Colored Population in reporting on the petition held that the evil complained of could not be prevented by legal means.[5] The position taken by this South Carolina committee evidently prevailed in the South. Georgia alone modified its slave code on the subject of miscegenation.[6]

The unsettled times also led to attempts to tighten existing restrictions relating to Negroes trading. Georgia, Texas, and Mississippi statutes forbade slaves to deal in or own certain property. A slave owner in Texas risked fine for permitting a slave to have any "pretended ownership or control over horses, cattle, sheep, or hogs." In Mississippi a master convicted of permitting a slave to "go at large and trade as a free man" could draw a fine of $500 and imprisonment for sixty days. Free Negroes were circumscribed in their business activity. A Virginia law forbade free Negroes as well as slaves to transport farm goods on a master's boat for purpose of sale. And in North Carolina free Negroes could not buy or hire slaves.[7]

Not all the new laws affecting Negroes in Southern States were of the character of the foregoing. Reform movements gained momentum in some areas and led to enactments intended to ameliorate the lot of the slave. The Alabama legislature ordered masters to provide counsel when slaves were indicted for any offense.[8] At the instigation of the governor and other citizens, a Georgia legislature repealed earlier laws forbidding the licensing of slaves or free Negroes to preach.[9] Texas constitutional amendments guaranteed trial by jury to slaves indicted for crimes of a "higher grade than petit larceny" and gave to the legislature power to enact laws enforcing humane treatment of slaves[10] James A. Lyon of Mississippi entered in his journal that he had drafted "an act regulating the marriage & parental relations existing between slaves." When his bill reached the Mississippi legislature, the Senate judiciary committee reported favorably on it, but held that time was not propitious for such a change. Lyon lamented to the civilized world the reluctance of lawmakers and concluded: "Perhaps God's intentions are to bring the institution to an absolute end."[11]

The Florida convention created special tribunals for free Negroes, slaves, and mulattoes. The special courts consisted of two justices and twelve citizens, slaveholders all. A majority of the court might pronounce judgment and could hold trials upon statement of offense in the warrant of arrest, without grand jury action. The Florida legislature modified the ordinance so that it applied to slaves, free Negroes, and mulattoes accused of capital crime.[12]

Preservation of order involved restraint of unruly whites

as well as Negroes. As an Arkansas resident said in 1861, there were "more dangers from bad white men among us than from the poor slaves."[13] Laws restricting the sale of liquor in certain localities and discouraging gambling sought to eliminate drinking and gambling as causes for breach of peace among whites. Mississippi tried to discourage another evil provocative of breach of peace by simplifying indictment for adultery and fornication.[14]

A survey of punishments in the states of the Confederacy shows that a medieval attitude toward crime and punishment existed. During the war, arson in South Carolina carried the death penalty. In Alabama theft of a horse, Negro, mare, gelding, colt, filly, or mule merited hanging. The Arkansas list of capital crimes included murder, arson, burglary, robbery, counterfeiting, forging, Negro stealing, embezzling public money, sodomy, kidnapping, perjury, subornation of perjury, bigamy, incest, and rape.[15]

As the war progressed, agencies for law enforcement became exceedingly unstable. Many local defense units seem to have engaged in law-breaking on their own. The Virginia Rangers were described as "organized bands of robbers and plunderers."[16] In a letter to the governor of North Carolina a citizen claimed that soldiers and home guards were "laying waist [sic] our country as fast as their hands can do it."[17] A Louisiana woman wrote her governor for protection against the "insults threats and outrages of the Prairie Rangers (Prairie Banditts [sic] would be a far more appropriate name) . . . We could not faire [sic] worse," she said, "were we surrounded by a band of Lincoln's mercenary hirelings."[18]

A serious hindrance to law and order lay in the problem of maintaining peace-time operation of the courts, particularly in areas threatened by enemy invasion. Occasionally it was necessary to pretermit court terms where "parties, witnesses, and solicitors" were away in state or Confederate defense. The approach of the enemy evoked from legislative bodies measures designed to circumvent the disruptive effects of invasion on the courts. When court houses became unsafe, legislatures authorized courts to move to other sites.

When counties were overrun, courts adjourned to other counties or judges transferred cases to other courts. When county newspapers closed shop for the duration, laws governing publication of legal notices were amended accordingly.[19] Legislatures attempted to prevent destruction of records by authorizing their removal from threatened sections. And when court papers were destroyed, elaborate machinery was set up for replacement by properly proved transcripts.[20]

Far more serious than the physical handicaps to regular court sessions, however, were the war-imposed absence of court officials, defendants, complainants, lawyers, witnesses, and jurors. In Mississippi amended laws permitted persons over sixty to serve as jurors and court clerks to practice law.[21] Florida, Mississippi, Alabama, Georgia, among others, provided for the absence of such officers as sheriffs, circuit clerks, chancery court registers, tax assessors, collectors, coroners, county surveyors, and probate judges.[22] In cases where defendants or plaintiffs were in the army, judges could suspend forfeiture of bond or grant a general continuance of the case.[23]

Although war brought to the courts litigation uncommon during tranquil times, it thrust into abeyance suits arising over debts. No state legislation during the war was more persistently demanded by the masses and more viciously execrated by minority and conservative opinion than that staying debts. A petition in South Carolina submitted from Charleston averred that a stay law would destroy the credit of merchants and, indeed, that of the state itself.[24] John W. Brown of Arkansas recorded in his diary, "The War and the Stay Law and hard times have suddenly done wonders on the moral sense of our people. Any excuse for failing to comply with obligation. Oh! for a spark of old time Honesty in our city and country."[25]

The Montgomery *Weekly Mail* saw no necessity for stay laws.[26] An Alabama legislator condemned the stay law proposed in the general assembly of his state in 1861 as "very objectionable."[27] The Selma *Reporter,* November 25, 1861, condemned the bill as "inadequate and repugnant."[28] The

Dallas *Herald* believed that such a law "would result in entire stagnation of business, a destruction of confidence and credit, an indifference to the fulfilment of just obligations."[29] The Texas *State Gazette* stated that the prairie country needed no relief and that the law would benefit only cotton growers. It predicted a demand for repeal within twelve months.[30]

The legislative papers of Tennessee contain petitions memorializing the state legislature to repeal its stay law, which was held to be "inexpedient and unjust." The Tennessee senate committee of the judiciary believed that the legislature had no constitutional right to prevent sale of personal property. A Tennessee journalist reported his impressions of the effects of the law:

> We now begin fully to realize the dreadful effects of this War of sections, this *Fratricidal War,* the horrors of which no imagination can depict. The Legislature proves itself even more corrupt than the people desire. . . . They enact stay laws impairing the obligations of contracts.[31]

The Raleigh *Standard* reported that convention opinion on the subject was adverse to the law.[32] After a stay law had passed the North Carolina legislature in 1861, James Gwyn of that state complained that ". . . everything [is] going to the dogs or rascals rather, stay law just in to their hand, poor chance for an honest man in this country now & I fear it will be wors [*sic*]."[33] Some Tar Heels in 1862 still clung to the hope that the North Carolina convention would "sink it into oblivion."[34]

Nowhere were expressions of pain over debtor relief more agonizing than in Louisiana. The *Daily Crescent* followed closely the progress of a Mississippi stay law in 1861 and concluded that the measure would destroy New Orleans' banks in two years. When a bill of the same nature came before the Louisiana legislature, this newspaper asked: "Is such legislation worthy of Louisiana's former honorable character?" The Shreveport *Semi-Weekly News* urged the governor to veto the stay law should it pass both houses. When the bill passed, the *Daily Crescent* moaned: "If ever a State has been more cursed than another by legislation, Louisiana is that state."[35]

In spite of opposition from merchants and lawyers and the press, legislatures in all the Confederate states passed stay laws and renewed them throughout the war period. The Lancaster, South Carolina, *Ledger*, never a convert to debtor relief, commented that the South Carolina legislature had responded to the "almost unanimous" will of the majority.[36] The same might have been said of other states in the South.

In Arkansas and South Carolina stay laws first gave protection to soldiers in state or Confederate service. Later extensions of the measure provided general debtor relief.[37] The Florida legislature moved to enact relief laws for debtors in 1861, but its action was repealed by the convention.[38] Governor Milton Perry urged the reenactment of a bill to prevent forced collections.[39] His legislators complied with a law affording protection until twelve months "after peace is made or until otherwise provided for by law . . . except by consent of defendant."[40] The Alabama debtor relief law of February, 1861, merely postponed collection for two terms of court.[41] The November legislature of the same year passed a measure for the duration of the war.[42]

Debtor relief in Georgia accompanied the suspension of specie payments. It was subsequently extended for the war.[43] Governor Pettus of Mississippi, in response to petitions, called a special legislative session to consider a stay law in July, 1861.[44] The law enacted by the Mississippi legislature suspended collection of debts and liabilities "on bonds, promissory notes, bills of exchange, open accounts, or contracts" for twelve months after the close of the war.[45]

The Waco *Southwest* predicted in January, 1861, that the "present excessive financial pressure will force enactment of laws suspending forced sales at ruinous sacrifices."[46] The Texas legislature in April, 1861, debated a bill allowing sales under court order provided the property was sold at two-third market value.[47] In the December, 1861, session controversial measures for relief to debtors were introduced. A senate bill would have closed the courts until six months after the war; and a house bill left courts open to suits but suspended sales of foreclosed property. A modification of the house bill passed. It suspended laws for collection of debts without delaying preliminary court proceedings. Subsequently the statute of limitations was abated as to debts and claims on bills, bonds, promissory notes, and all contracts for the payment of money.[49]

The North Carolina stay law was the subject of more than ordinary controversy. Passed in May, 1861, it was declared unconstitutional by the state supreme court and repealed at the next special session of the legislature, only to be repassed later.[50]

Governor Moore of Louisiana cautioned against dealing a blow to "public or private credit."[51] The Louisiana law governing sales under executions required that the buyer's offer for the property equal the appraised value as of the first of April, 1861. Otherwise the sale had to await the end of the war and twelve months thereafter.[52]

Tennessee and Virginia completed the roll of states providing debtor relief. The first Tennessee law was perhaps the most radical of all in that judges were requested not to hold courts for twelve months for cases involving debts and money.[53] A later act demanded that property sold for debt bring three-fourths of the market value.[54] Virginia ordinances merely prevented sacrifice of property by forced sale.[55] The historian of Confederate courts concludes that despite the reduction of court cases resulting from these stay laws and suspension of statutes of limitation, the courts were "surprisingly active everywhere, not even excepting Tennessee."[56]

Although Tennessee's courts continued to function with some semblance of regularity, her governor and legislature went into eclipse after Federal occupation of Nashville in February and Memphis in June, 1862, Governor Isham Harris and the Tennessee legislators had taken refuge in Memphis after evacuating their capital; and the legislature convened there on February 20, 1862. After adjournment, Harris fled to the Army of Tennessee.[57] Tennessee was then bereft of its legislative and executive branches of government. An attempt to go through the formality of a state election in 1863 necessitated establishing polls in regiments, rather than in precincts.[58] Judge Robert L. Caruthers was elected to succeed Harris, but he did not take over the duties of office. From his position behind Confederate lines Governor Harris continued to direct what little state business remained.[59]

Four other states shared with Tennessee the difficulties of legislatures on the run. When Sherman's army left Atlanta in November, 1864, and turned toward Milledgeville, Governor Brown and the Georgia legislature evacuated the latter city. The last session of the Georgia legislature during the life of the Confederacy convened at Macon in February and March, 1865.[60] Mississippi legislators also knew the vicissitudes of fugitive sessions. The spring and summer called session, 1864, met of necessity in Macon, Mississippi, rather than at the capital at Jackson. And the year 1865 found the lawmakers seeking safety a scant thirty miles from Macon at Columbus, Mississippi.[61]

The peregrinations of the Louisiana general assembly proved equally unsettling. When General Benjamin Butler took over New Orleans in May, 1862, Baton Rouge, the state capital, became uncomfortably vulnerable. Opelousas was a temporary refuge for state offices and for the legislative session of 1862-1863. Then the government moved its headquarters to Shreveport, where it remained until the end of the war.[62] After Little Rock fell to the Federals in 1863, the Arkansas legislature held only one last session which convened at Washington, Arkansas, in 1864.[63]

State general assemblies, whether firmly ensconced in impregnable capitals or meeting in out-of-the-way places, were deeply concerned with maintenance of civil government. They did not fail to make provision for elections under all sorts of unusual circumstances or for the holding over of offices when elections were not feasible. In Mississippi special legislation of 1864 enabled Yazoo City officials to continue their duties until the next regular election.[64] The Arkansas legislature provided for polls in military camps for those counties and districts occupied by the enemy.[65]

Georgia, North Carolina, Texas, and Virginia lawmakers took similar action.[66]

Most of the state governments seemed more concerned with economic and military and political activities than they were about cultural affairs. Education systems felt profoundly the disruptive effects of civil war. North Carolina was the only Confederate state that had made conspicuous progress toward a public school system, but all states had provided grants before the war to supplement county funds for educational purposes. During the war, however, defense needs made heavy inroads into these funds.

Georgia laws had permitted counties to establish public schools, to draw an amount from the state for their support, and to levy a tax for educational purposes. Beginning in 1861, the legislature permitted some counties to divert their school funds for soldier relief or for purchase of necessitous goods.[67] But the state educational fund continued to serve throughout the war as a source of income for county schools when not allocated by special legislation for other purposes.[68]

The financial plan of the comptroller of Texas incited some newspaper comment. The Dallas *Herald* disapproved the diversion of school funds to the state treasury. The *State Gazette* explained that the school fund, $2,000,000, was to remain intact; that the comptroller was to take from the fund only those proceeds arising from future sales of public land.[69] In 1864 the *Confederate News* exposed what it considered a fraud against the school fund. Railroads had borrowed sizeable sums from the fund at attractive interest rates. Now, when gold and silver were at a premium, the legislature had passed a bill permitting railroads to discharge their school debt in state treasury warrants, the market value of which was six to ten cents on the dollar.[70]

In Louisiana the legislature made a slight reduction of its pro rata apportionment for each educable child in the state.[71] The state superintendent of education, Henry Avery, asked that his duties be extended to consolidate the administration of schools.[72] The general assembly did not support his proposal and in 1865 eliminated his office.[73] In the meantime the need for money forced the legislators to transfer

$200,000 of the Free School Accumulating Fund to the state general operating fund.[74] Still appropriations continued for school support; and in 1865 the general assembly voted $100,000 for school books offered at cost to parish children who could pay for them and free to others.[75]

In Confederate Mississippi common schools fared better than colleges. Here, as in other states, a general educational fund was divided among the counties which might levy a tax for school support. And here, also, the educational picture varied with the wealth and culture of local citizenry. The Mississippi legislature, which in antebellum times had left the establishment and maintenance of schools to the initiative of the counties, now gave to some counties, by special legislation, the privilege of using school funds for war purposes.[76]

North Carolina had a stalwart champion of public schools in Calvin Henderson Wiley, its superintendent of education. Even so, legislation of 1861 reflected the general abatement of interest in this aspect of culture. The general assembly repealed a law requiring county courts to collect taxes for common schools and left the matter to the discretion of the justices.[77] In June of 1861 a convention delegate suggested that the schools be suspended for the war and school revenue diverted to defense.[78] Countering such schemes, Wiley began a propaganda drive for maintaining school funds intact and keeping schools in operation.[79] Because he had the support of Governor Vance, the North Carolina school system weathered the crisis though with an ever-diminishing roster of male students; and in 1864 North Carolina school legislation took on new life. An act passed in December broadened the base of the system by permitting any district in the state to establish a graded school.[80]

Certainly the efforts of state governments to preserve basic institutions were not entirely fruitless. When withdrawal of men into state and Confederate defense units first weakened patrol systems, state laws attempted to tighten controls over Negroes and to keep insubordination, disloyalty, and violence at a minimum. Remarkably, no major slave insurrection took place; and murderous assaults by Negroes on white men or women were rare. The degree to which the amended state slave codes and enforcement procedures merited credit for the relative calm among the Negro population is conjectural. There is also to be considered the fact that most Southern states were not completely denuded of man-power and arms by Confederate needs; that most Southern states retained some organized state forces to deploy against threats of insurrection, at least for the greater part of the war years. At any rate, available records of the period leave the impression that lawlessness among whites was more common than violence among the Negroes. Both civil and military authority apparently failed to arrest the wave of disorder throughout the South among unstable elements of white society.

Nevertheless, the legal system and machinery of civil government continued to function, and these political institutions resumed normality with remarkable celerity once the war ended. Even the school systems, never very robust, survived the stagnation and privation of war times. Although war arrested their progress, they continued in most Southern states to draw enough financial support to insure their continued operations.

★

VI

MORALE

IN THEIR ATTEMPTS to promote security at home and to insure economic and institutional stability, Southern state legislatures enacted programs which followed well-defined objectives. Laws sustaining soldier and civilian morale, on the other hand, usually grew out of economic or political or defense measures. It was often incidental, sometimes accidental, when acts designed for other purposes served to stimulate soldier *esprit de corps* and civilian determination to sustain the cause of Southern independence.

Several states made tremendous efforts until the closing days of the war to insure a supply of clothing and blankets for soldiers in the field. The states' efforts doubtless discouraged defeatism among soldiers; but the service, begun as a military necessity, continued only because of Confederate inability to care properly for the men. Soldiers' pay elicited comment from state governments. But resolutions dealing with pay often cited the destitution of soldiers' families as an economic reason for the need for prompt Confederate action.[1] Southern states relieved soldiers from forced sales for debts; and some exempted soldiers from poll taxes and property taxes.[2] These relief laws exhibited a spirit of fairness which probably stimulated volunteering; but their passage almost uniformly preceded the existence of a severe morale problem.

Proposals to permit absentee voting by soldiers may have arisen from concern for morale. It is equally possible that by such proposals ensconced legislators sought access to that same majority which had seated them before army service had disrupted the local political balance. At any rate, North Carolina, Florida, Virginia, South Carolina, Georgia, and Mississippi allowed service men stationed beyond the state to participate in state elections.[3] The Alabama legislature granted the privilege to soldiers in the Confederate election of 1861, but did not renew the concession in later elections.[4] The Montgomery *Weekly Advertiser* complained to its readers that the judiciary committees of both houses were "solicitous that the soldiers should be authorized to vote . . . but the conclusion was reached that it could not be done," for constitutional reasons. The *Advertiser* thought that the soldiers would doubtless feel "comparatively indifferent" to the deprivation.[5]

Controversy arose in Texas also over the constitutionality of soldier voting outside the state. The *State Gazette* thought that the state could not "disfranchise her citizens by ordering them out of her limits, nor deprive them of any of the privileges of citizenship." Apparently, the legislature did not agree, since in 1863, Governor Lubbock was still vainly trying to obtain legislative approval of a bill enabling Texas soldiers to vote anywhere in the Confederacy.[7]

Whether the laws extending soldier voting privileges beyond their states appreciably enhanced morale is conjectural. State legislation providing aid for sick and wounded soldiers, however, definitely stemmed from morale as well as humanitarian motives and definitely stimulated morale among the armed forces. The Louisiana legislature appropriated money for state hospitals for service men and incorporated an association for relief of the sick and wounded which received substantial state support.[8]

The North Carolina legislature ordered the governor to send a surgeon to Virginia to purchase supplies for the sick and to establish a hospital. It set aside $300,000 for agents and surgeons to provide for the wants of North Carolina soldiers hospitalized in Virginia.[9] The legislature further resolved in 1864 that the surgeon general of the state should work for the transfer of the North Carolina wounded to hospitals in the home state.[10]

Arkansas sold bonds for sick, wounded, and disabled volunteers and for soldiers' homes and hospitals at several places in the state.[11] Texas appropriated money in 1862 and 1863 for aid to the sick, but it did not utilize the funds. An act of December, 1863, repealed former appropriations and set up a fund of $200,000 "to be administered as the Governor may deem necessary." The legislature also directed the governor to send a commissioner to Arkansas and Louisiana to relieve destitute Texas soldiers in those states.[12]

Florida provided money for wayside homes for her itinerant sick and wounded and for aid to those confined in hospitals in Richmond and elsewhere.[13] Virginia produced an educational plan for her citizens discharged from service on account of wounds. They could receive a "full course of instruction at the university, without charge for tuition, use of laboratories, lecture rooms, public halls or dormitories."[14]

Care of Georgia's sick and wounded was in the hands of the Georgia Relief and Hospital Association, to which the Georgia general assembly gave $200,000 in 1861 and $500,000 in 1863.[15] Alabama soldiers received zealous attention from the state legislature for the first three years of war. An Alabama agent, Arthur Francis Hopkins, and his wife supervised the state's hospitals in Virginia for Alabama casualties.[16] Appropriations to the Virginia hospitals and those in Alabama were liberal until an act in December, 1863, repealed all laws for relief of Alabamians in Virginia. Other military aid societies and wayside homes continued to receive state funds throughout 1864.[17]

Mississippi began to care for her sick and wounded in 1861, when the legislature provided for agents and hospitals at suitable cities outside the state.[18] The legislature authorized the governor to appoint medical commissioners to examine Mississippi's soldiers in hospitals and to attend to their needs.[19] A surgeon in Lee's corps wrote in 1864 that Mississippians were being neglected by "their friends at home." This observer felt that the poor organization of relief societies in the state had discouraged appropriations and private contributions.[20]

State legislators were consciously engaging in attempts to build morale when they sought to encourage their soldiers by lavish praise and by assurance of state responsibility for the families back home. Southern politicians evidently believed profoundly in the efficacy of resolutions avowing gratitude and often accompanied them with instructions for transmittal to men in the field.[21] Georgia on occasions gave medals as well as praise to her brave men.[22] Several states established departments or commissions of army records. The Alabama, Louisiana, and Mississippi legislatures placed a superintendent in charge of collecting the names of all officers and soldiers from those states.[23] Alabama, North Carolina, and Florida laws called for a roll of honor; and in Florida the governor received instructions to distribute among the soldiers one thousand copies of the act pertaining to an honor roll for deceased officers and soldiers.[24] A Georgia law authorized a register for all participating in service and a "suitable monument" for those who died.[25] The Louisiana general assembly appropriated money to purchase copies of the *Army and Navy Messenger,* a periodical published in Shreveport, Louisiana, for its soldiers.[26]

Soldiers were not the sole recipients of expressions of appreciation. The women of the Confederacy received the plaudits of state governments, who commended them for their support of the war effort. Legislative bodies were aware of the importance of the women in sustaining morale and acknowledged through join resolutions feminine "zeal and directed energies."[27] As a matter of fact, the engendering of home front morale, among women and other civilians, was the especial province of state legislatures.

The states' attempts to maintain locally the will to fight and to endure led state legislators into extensive welfare legislation and some market controls. Appeals for price controls began to flow into state governors' offices in the spring of 1861. A disgruntled Georgia woman wrote to Governor Brown: "It appears that all the poor from here has gone. . . . Our kind friends that has remained that no one member of their families has gone and sell things to the soldiers families just as high as he would to those that have their all. I do not think it is right."[28] The Montgomery *Weekly Mail* cautioned the legislators to protect soldiers against the "vultures" which follow in the wake of an army to "fatten on its necessities!"[29]

Georgia, Alabama, North Carolina, Florida, Mississippi, Texas, and South Carolina responded sooner or later to such appeals; but invariably anti-extortion and anti-monopoly laws were vaguely worded and susceptible to evasion. A year after Georgia controls went into effect, Governor Brown complained that the law ". . . has proved almost a dead letter upon the Statute books . . . If a single conviction has yet been had, I have not been informed of it."[30] The Savannah *Daily Morning News* accused speculators of holding immense quantities of foodstuff from the market.[31] The *Confederate Union* named the South's conquering foes as Southern distillers, cotton planters, government agents, and speculators.[32] Legislators in Georgia were still, as Joseph Addison Turner put it, "hammering away at the problem of regulating prices" in 1864, and they never came up with any effective plan of control.[33]

The story of Alabama's restraints upon extortioners was similar. The law there forbade monopolies in livestock but left definition of the deed subject to court interpretation.[34] The governor of Alabama frankly admitted that he was unable to control speculation with existing legal machinery.[35] A revised and strengthened Alabama law, which permitted a profit of fifteen to twenty per cent, depending on the commodity, likewise failed to stop extortionate price levels. In 1863 Major L. T. Wright wrote the governor that officers would find it difficult to keep their units together when the soldiers learned that their families were being "so put upon."[36]

The heavy drain on North Carolina's resources by troops concentrated in nearby Virginia necessitated early action in that state to prevent a severe shortage of food. The governor applied an embargo on essentials and the North Carolina convention followed with an ordinance denouncing speculation in specified articles.[37] In 1862 Governor Henry T. Clark urged the convention to pass a maximum price law.[38] At the recommendation of the convention's president, the new governor, Vance, left the problem to the legislature, which was to meet in regular session in the winter months of 1862.[39] The Raleigh *Register* and other papers expressed the hope that the legislature would take the matter in hand. "It is an act of madness," the *Register* stated, "to stop and split hairs on legal or constitutional points when the life of the nation hangs trembling in the balance."[40] The legislature continued the policy of the North Carolina convention, that of an embargo on necessitous goods.[41]

The Florida general assembly passed an embargo act in 1861 and withheld food products from export trade. The act set a limit of thirty-three per cent on profits in essential food items.[42] The price controls were short-lived as the Florida convention, meeting in January, 1862, repealed the law.[43] An anti-monopoly law of December, 1861, was weakened by the difficulty or perhaps unwillingness on the part of the courts to enforce the law. A new measure in 1862 penalized false representation and monopoly for the purpose of raising prices and required that goods purchased outside the state be offered at local market prices.[44]

Florida's Governor John Milton believed that the practice of blockade-running benefitted local speculators and their Yankee partners more than Floridians. He contended that outgoing cotton made its way directly to Northern markets.[45] By 1863 Milton had swung his legislators around to disapproval of the trade; and his general assembly urged that congress consider laws to confine the import-export trade to state and central government operations. The resolutions stated that "The exportation of cotton, tobacco, and other products from the Confederate States by private enterprise, and for private emoluments, tends to depreciate the currency, to corrupt public morals, to lessen the production of food and otherwise to injure the cause for which we are fighting."[46]

The Richmond *Enquirer* in 1862 expressed a contrary opinion. The newspaper praised the "merchants, manufacturers and artizans, who, in the pressure brought on us by the blockade, have exerted their energies, taxed their ingenuity, and risked their capital, to introduce into our market articles of necessity or of convenience, though they have sold them at high prices."[47] The Richmond *Dispatch* took the view that money, not extortion, was the root of Confederate disaster. "Improve the currency," it said, "and the extortioners will fail."[48] The Virginia legislature considered price control in 1863; and a Virginia diarist who disapproved of the proposal described it as ruinous. "It fills me with terror to think of the effect on this City," he said, ". . . Production and movement will be so cut off and curtailed that there will be great danger of famine here."[49] The Richmond *Enquirer* looked upon the bill as a "dangerous experiment—simply the old Law of Maximum revived." Like the *Dispatch,* the *Enquirer* laid extortion at the door of a redundant currency and blamed current distress upon failure to make use of cotton and other products as media of exchange.[50]

Mississippi, Texas, Arkansas, and Tennessee either made only feeble moves to control speculation or took no action at all, although the problem was as acute in these states as elsewhere. The Nashville *Patriot* reported a rumor in 1861 that a combination of men was planning to buy up flour and wheat and raise prices.[51] John W. Brown of Arkansas described the situation in his state thus:

But little doing now except army affairs . . . and the activity of the speculators, who are everywhere on the alert, and who show a disposition so strong for vast profits that they could sell the blood of the soldiers and their families if price enough was offered, and what looks worst of all, most of them are the rampant men—who were tumultuous for Secession."[52]

And in Texas a letter from B. L. Peel to the governor states that "Texas has been swarming with a set of sharp speculators. . . . We must be protected or these Shylocks will starve us. . . . Stop them—stop them at once."[53]

Mississippi's law made speculation in necessities subject to a fine of $1000 and/or a maximum jail sentence of one year.[54] The Texas laws to control speculation first concentrated on those fraudulently buying under pretense of state or Confederate commission, or those who, as state or Confederate agents, profited personally from purchase and resale.[55] Governor Lubbock insisted that extortion had to be more effectively restricted, but he left solutions up to the legislature.[56] The Texas general assembly later required persons buying beef or butchering beef for market to file information with the county clerks regarding their operations; but this was as far as the legislature went in enacting controls over speculation.[57] The *Tri-Weekly Telegraph* defended the legislators and warned that "As great a tyrant and as great a despot may be set up by the Legislature as by any other power." The paper stated further that most of the goods in the speculative market were non-essential commodities.[58]

Repeated petitions reached the governor and legislature of South Carolina from persons seeking relief from scarcity and high prices. Spartanburg citizens complained that manufacturers were sending cotton cloth out of the state or selling at an enormous price to planters who could get only seven cents per pound for their cotton.[59] Other petitioners called attention to the cost of salt, bacon, and other necessities.[60] Until 1863, however, the legislature maintained the position that prices should be left to the natural law of supply and demand. In the meantime, speculation had aroused one citizen to remark: "My country—oh, my country—men instead of fighting the enemy are robbing each other."[61] And a South Carolina wag penned a thirty-line poem on speculation which ended dramatically:

> O, righteous Rope why dost thou sleep?
> While orphans, widows, Devils weep?
> And crime in black confusion roll
> O'er our dear country's troubled soul?[62]

When pressure finally brought about the passage of a measure controlling "exorbitant or unreasonable rates or prices," it was left to the jury to determine what constituted "exorbitant or unreasonable" profit.[63] In the spring of 1863, the legislature authorized the governor to proclaim embargoes on provisions at his discretion. Enforcement of this act produced some complaints of hardship, but the trend toward high prices was abated little, if at all.[64]

The failure of the South Carolina laws to prevent unreasonable advance in prices matched the inadequacy of

legislative controls in other states. But states whose law-
makers could not or would not apply strictures to speculation could and would vote relief for its victims. This relief
was "practical" politics.

The first relief laws provided support for the indigent
families of service men. The pattern followed during 1861
left to counties or tax districts the responsibility for raising
necessary funds by taxation.[65] Since relief was most drastically
needed in poor or invaded areas, funds had to come from
insufficient sources of revenue. Letters to governors and to
newspapers in 1862 told of severe want and distress among
the poorer classes of people in the poorer counties or tax
districts.[66]

Georgia answered Governor Brown's request for relief
with a $2,500,000 fund for support of indigent widows and
orphans of soldiers and families of service men. The state
set aside another $300,000 for the evacuation of indigent non-
combatants in the line of invasion.[67]

Arkansas and Louisiana provided an allotment system for
needy families, and the former state authorized an agent to
buy corn for families of frontier counties.[68] North Carolina
appropriated $1,000,000 for those service families who needed
assistance and set up a plan for purchase of provisions by a
central bureau for distribution among the poor.[69] Other
states allocated varying amounts for this purpose.[70]

Long before the original sums provided had been ex-
pended, governors began to urge further consideration of
ways and means to mitigate the distress among families of
soldiers.[71] Since local agencies had found it difficult to purchase needed provisions, legislators studied distribution problems along with proposals to increase former appropriations
for the needy.

The South Carolina legislature supplemented its appropriation of $500,000 with a two per cent tax in kind paid by
"producers in any district or parish when required by the
Board of Relief."[72]

The Mississippi legislature required boards of police in
the several counties to prepare a roll of all soldiers in Con-

federate or militia service, a copy of which was to be sent to the auditor of public accounts. Each county received a share of the state relief fund in proportion to the number of its needy. Boards of police could receive, in lieu of money, produce yielded by a state tax-in-kind. County sheriffs could impress supplies if necessary, under the authorization of the boards.[73] Virginia lagged somewhat behind other states in that her 1863 relief laws left to the discretion of county courts the aid given to indigent soldiers and their families. Virginia laws did, however, give county courts the right to impress provisions for the needy.[74]

As need for relief mounted in 1864 and 1865, difficulties in securing provisions became almost insurmountable. The Georgia governor bought wagons and teams to transport state-purchased corn to soldiers' families in need; and the legislature commended his action.[75] When the regular session of the legislature convened in 1864, the legislators provided for the purchase of corn to be distributed to needy families throughout the state. Governor Brown could impress rolling stock for the transportation of the supplies for the indigent.[76] Throughout the last meeting of Georgia legislators the state continued to provide relief to soldiers' families, making special arrangements to aid those exiled before the advance of Sherman's army.[77]

The governor of Louisiana asked for and received legislative approval to attempt some sort of arrangement with Confederate authorities whereby needy soldiers' families could draw rations from the army, upon payment of cost by the state government.[78] Louisiana not only made money appropriations to the indigent during the last trying months of the war, but purchased corn and other foods for them.[79]

The administration of relief laws in Texas suffered from the conscription of local officials.[80] Procurement of supplies with depreciated money presented another, acute problem in that state.[81] The Florida legislature, confronted by a shortage of provisions for the needy, asked the Confederate government to release from impressment the supplies required for local consumption.[82] Virginia began suddenly in 1864

to show unwonted energy and provided a relief fund of
$1,000,000. The legislature of the Old Dominion also em-
powered sheriffs to summon a posse to enforce impressments
for families of soldiers or their widows or orphans.[83]

Alabama increased its appropriations for relief in 1864.
The laws permitted county sheriffs to employ wagons, teams,
and drivers to carry subsistence articles purchased for indigent. If funds were insufficient, county commissioners could
also levy an additional tax.[84]

In Mississippi relief commissioners had similar authority
to impress teams and wagons for transportation of supplies
to the indigent.[85] Just before the end of the war, the Mississippi legislators arrived at a policy which was, at least on
paper, the most far-reaching measure of its kind enacted
by any state during the war. The law provided for a tax of
two per cent in kind on corn, wheat, bacon, leather, woollen,
and cotton fabrics, with necessary exemptions for home use;
a further tax of 15 per cent on the regular state tax; and a
tax of two per cent on gross profits of iron foundaries, machine shops, sawmills, blacksmiths, shoemakers, and other
tradesmen and speculators. The beneficiaries of the act
were divided into three classes: those entirely dependent,
those deficient in breadstuffs, and those deficient in bacon.[86]

Scarcity of provisions created everywhere difficulties for
relief agencies. But in instances, certain articles were at once
so necessary and so rare as to require special attention on the
part of the states. This was true of cloth, yarn, cotton and
woollen cards; of salt; and of medicines. Alabama law-makers
directed county commissioners to pay for medicines used in
treating indigent families of soldiers.[87] Louisiana legislators
set aside $500,000 for medicine for all needy persons and
established a state laboratory to manufacture and dispense
medicines.[88]

County commissioners in Alabama were authorized to
manufacture salt for those in poverty-stricken circumstances,
and the state relief agency was to distribute salt among
counties in amounts proportionate to the number of in-
digents.[89] In Mississippi the legislature ordered $500,000 to

be used to purchase salt for needy families of soldiers.[90] In Arkansas a salt agent was appointed to buy the commodity for distribution among the destitute.[91]

Several state legislatures recognized the importance of furnishing the poor with cotton cards. The Florida governor was granted $30,000 to buy cards for distribution among the poor.[92] Texas citizens requested the governor's aid in relieving a shortage of cloth in 1862. Penitentiary-manufactured cloth was available to families of soldiers in the Lone Star State, but the procedure of distribution was involved and susceptible to mismanagement.[93] The legislature attempted to make more cloth available in 1864 by dividing the state into districts which contained approximately the same number of indigent families of servicemen. Among the districts there was to be an annual distribution of 600,000 yards of cloth with thread.[94] The Arkansas legislature directed the governor of that state to buy and distribute cotton and woollen cards, drugs, medicines for the poor and paper for county officials.[95] Louisiana made frequent appropriations for cards, and Mississippi, Georgia, and Alabama legislatures made substantial provisions for these articles for the families of soldiers.[96]

Developments in the South from 1862 on indicate that direct or indirect programs to sustain morale among soldiers and civilians were something less than successful. The thoroughly documented studies of desertion in the Confederate army and disloyalty on the home front give ample proof of that fact.[97] Contemporary comments emphasize the general inadequacy of the states' attempts to clothe and equip their troops, with North Carolina the exception, and recount descriptions of the woeful shortages of many items required for soldier comfort and recovery. And as for the protestations of appreciation from state governments, most soldiers would doubtless have gladly exchanged these for a full knapsack or sturdy shoes.

Evidence further highlights the ineffectiveness of price controls. The states which made gestures toward speculation and extortion were evasive in the nature of regulations. Their legislators railed against the evils but defined them in such terms as to leave enforcement agencies stymied in their evaluation of evidence as conclusive proof of the offense.

When southern legislatures turned to relief programs to correct the effects of speculation and extortion, there they confronted shortages of necessitous goods and inefficiency, sometimes dishonesty, in distributive and administrative agencies. The inadequacy of existing transportation facilities made for an unequal distribution of farm produce and manu- factured goods, with many areas suffering greatly while an abundance prevailed in others. Furthermore, the absence of a well-designed system, with the authority of participating agencies clearly defined, all too frequently left the dispensing of aid to the discretion of incompetent or dishonest county officials.

★

VII

STATE REVENUE

A HISTORIAN OF SOUTH CAROLINA during the Civil War asserts that financial problems there were negligible.[1] This boast could not be made for other Southern states. The South's economy had a credit base lying outside its boundaries. Within, it had no "great accumulations of cash or credit" upon which to draw.[2] The chief resource, cotton, lost its market early in the war; and expenses for local defense, direct and indirect participation in trading and manufacturing, relief and morale measures made increased revenue essential in financing new functions of government. In these circumstances war financing in the confederated states became a real challenge. Legislatures had to choose between taxation and the loan and paper currency methods of acquiring funds. The first involved the risk of stifling business enterprise important to the war effort; and the second imposed the hazard of encouraging speculation and inflation, with bankrupty being an ultimate possibility. Hope of a short war led Southern states to the second method.[3]

For a time, loans, usually in the form of bonds, were favored as a more sound revenue source than unlimited treasury note issues. Unfortunately, the market for state bonds contracted as confidence in Confederate success dwindled; hence resort to the bond mode of raising revenue decreased markedly in the latter years of the conflict.

Alabama financial legislation of 1861 called for specific loans up to $2,100,000 and other bond issues to meet any deficiencies that might occur in the treasury.[4] In 1862, the governor received authority to borrow at a rate not to exceed eight per cent and for a period not to exceed six months.[5] The general assembly continued the policy of permitting bond sales to meet treasury deficiencies until 1864, at which time the bonded indebtedness stood at $5,521,500, over half of which represented the bond sales of 1861.[6]

The Arkansas legislature provided for $2,000,000 in war bonds in 1861.[7] It is not surprising that Tennessee's bond issue of $5,000,000, voted in the first year of war, was the volunteer state's one recourse to this revenue medium, since the state was soon occupied by Federal troops.[8] Florida, too, abandoned borrowing in the form of bond sales after initial ventures into the sale of $500,000 in interest-bearing certificates.[9] In December, 1861, the Florida legislators permitted authorities to offer unsold certificates to the state's creditors willing to accept them.[10] The treasurer's report in 1864 stated that only $300,000 of the bonds had been disposed of.[11]

Georgia's general assembly in 1860 gave the governor power to negotiate sale of six per cent bonds to supply money for military preparations.[12] Pressure was brought to bear upon the chief executive for seven per cent bonds, and a letter from Governor Brown to R. R. Cuyler of the Central Railroad and Banking Company in April, 1861, promised cooperation.[13] The Georgia legislature in December passed a bill enabling the governor to issue bonds or treasury notes, the bonds to carry not more than eight per cent interest. The governor received discretionary authority to obtain money for purchase or manufacture of arms by either selling bonds for the entire amount appropriated for the purpose or by issuing state treasury notes for part of the cost.[14]

By this time, divergence of opinion had arisen between Governor Brown and leading bankers of the state. Writing again to R. R. Cuyler, Brown with characteristic bluntness states his preference for note issues to finance military operations and his intention to use bonds for the Confederate war tax.[15]

Louisiana borrowed heavily from state banks during the first year of war. It was not until 1862 that the legislature passed financial measures permitting sale of bonds totaling first $1,000,000 and later $7,000,000.[16] By 1864, $74,000 of the first issue remained unsold, and $225,000 authorized under the second act had found no buyers.[17] The Louisiana legislature ordered sale of another bond issue in 1864, this time in amount of $10,000,000 but bonds were purchased with Confederate or state treasury notes. Treasury notes on deposit with the state were to be cancelled in amounts equal to sums realized from the bond sale.[18] The Shreveport *Semi-Weekly News* complimented the law as a "settled determination on the part of the state to redeem its issues of treasury notes."[19] Only $571,940 of these bonds had been disposed of by January, 1865.[20]

The secession convention in Mississippi cleared the way for bond issues by amending its constitution removing restrictions from borrowing.[21] The first bond law permitted circulation of ten per cent certificates up to $1,000,000.[22] At the end of the year, the state had sold only $34,360 of the bonds.[23] In August, 1864, Governor Charles Clark asked for an issue of state treasury notes to meet current expenses. Instead, his legislature ordered a sale of $2,000,000 in eight per cent bonds and, that failing, a note issue.[24] Faith in Mississippi's securities was not such as to sustain the bonds on the market.

North Carolina's bonded indebtedness for war effort began in 1861 when convention and legislature voted loans totaling $10,250,000.[25] The state's bonds in 1862 brought high figures ranging from par to 129.[26] In 1863 the legislature authorized sale of six per cent bonds in amount of $2,000,000 and in 1864, of $3,000,000.[27] The legislature provided for no further issue other than bonds allocated for purpose of refunding bonds, paying loans due or redeeming treasury notes. The treasury's report at the end of the war stated that North Carolina's $1000 bonds brought $74 in specie in 1864.[28]

The South Carolina legislature ordered the first loans in December and January of 1860-1861, and the last in December, 1861.[29] The general assembly provided during this period for issues of $3,375,000 in bonds, only $2,402,639 of which were sold.[30] In 1863, before Vicksburg and Gettysburg, South Carolina's bonds were quoted at 127 on the market.[31]

Frontier defense in Texas necessitated a bond sale in

March, 1861.[32] Later in the year the legislature directed the governor to execute up to $1,000,000 in eight per cent bonds.[33] The governor commissioned E. B. Nichols to sell them.[34] When the bonds had not been placed on the market by January of 1862, the legislature gave the governor, comptroller, and treasury authority to appoint agents to negotiate the sale of Texas bonds.[35] Texas credit, however, apparently carried little weight in the financial world since the bonds in time dropped to a value of one-fourth of par value. The state then attempted to sell its United States five per cent Texas indemnity bonds, but the possibility of Federal repudiation frustrated attempts to make the most effective use of these bonds for war-time needs.[36] The last state bonds authorized were in amount of $2,000,000 and could be paid for in cotton.[37]

Virginia began the war with a heavy bonded indebtedness which rendered further bond sales impracticable. Consequently her bonded indebtedness increased only slightly in 1861; even so, it reached a figure of $33,000,000.[38]

As bonds sales proved ephemeral sources of revenue, a trend developed toward increase in circulation of state treasury notes. Alabama issued her first treasury notes in 1861.[39] But opposition to the policy was so strong there in 1862 that a bill providing for circulation of $2,000,000 notes passed by a slim majority of four votes.[40] By 1864, however, the legislature was permitting the governor unlimited note issues as needed to meet appropriations and debts.[41] Arkansas' earliest treasury notes were interest-bearing. In 1862, the legislature ordered that no further payment of interest accrue on treasury warrants issued after passage of the act.[42] Demands for increased supply of small change notes were met by laws requiring that given percentages of treasury warrants issued be in amounts of twenty-five and fifty cents and $1.[43]

When the Florida general assembly legalized printing of $500,000 in treasury notes, it guaranteed that notes of banks receiving state currency at par would be honored by all officers charged with collecting state revenue.[44] The legislature in session in December, 1862, authorized a further issue of $300,000.[45] Other note issues followed for such specific purposes as the Confederate war tax and relief. The total amount authorized by Florida was $2,450,000, most of which had been actually circulated by 1865.[46]

Governor Joseph E. Brown early evinced a partiality for paper money as a solution to Georgia's financial problems.[47] Consequently, in this state legislative issues of treasury notes rather than bonds became the rule. In 1862 and 1863, laws provided for $2,000,000 in notes in denominations of $4 and less.[48] Georgia's paper currency authorized during the war reached a total figure of $13,739,500.[49]

Louisiana's first financial measure of the war permitted the governor to obtain revenue either by bonds or treasury notes or both. The law limited currency to $2,000,000 of the total of $7,000,000 provided for.[50] In the next year the governor received authority to print paper money in amount not to exceed $20,000,000. Subsequent legislation required the governor to cease issuing notes when sale of bonds became sufficient to pay expenses.[51] Governor Henry Watkins Allen provided a partial solution for depreciating paper currency by establishing state stores where scarce articles could be bought for Louisiana treasury notes.[52]

The state of Mississippi began the year 1861 with $1,000,000 in treasury notes to meet the defense budget.[53] The state legislature allocated $5,000,000 in December, 1861, to be issued to farmers as advances on cotton.[54] These cotton notes competed somewhat with the Confederate Produce Loan of May, 1861, but they provided a currency based on a product which was described as otherwise "dead capital."[55] Additional treasury notes in the amount of $2,500,000 were authorized in 1862.[56] The 1862 issue, with bank notes, railroad, and other corporation notes sufficed until 1864; in the summer of that year, however, the governor warned of the need for additional treasury notes.[57] The legislature, although partially acceding to his request, required that he first attempt to sell bonds in the amount of $2,000,000 at eight per cent interest and to print currency only up to the difference in value of the bonds sold and the $2,000,000 needed.[58]

Both convention and legislature in North Carolina enacted financial measures in the early war period.[59] By September,

1861, circulation of treasury notes had reached the figure of $3,357,810.50.[60] The legislature approved printing of an additional $4,800,000 in September and December, 1961, and the convention authorized still another issue of $2,000,000 in May, 1862.[61] Although one newspaper expressed the hope that the legislature would not overissue treasury notes, the December, 1862, session of the general assembly provided for another $1,500,000 in treasury notes which could be funded in six per cent coupon bonds.[62] An act of 1863 limited the total amount of treasury notes in circulation at any one time to $6,500,000.[63] The last note issue authorized was for $3,000,000, bringing the gross amount of treasury notes authorized in North Carolina up to a total of $9,500,000.[64]

South Carolina's financial policy was less expansive than that of North Carolina. The Bank of the State of South Carolina was permitted to issue $200,000 in notes during 1861 and $500,000 during 1863.[65] The city of Charleston circulated up to $300,000 under act of the legislature.[66] Otherwise South Carolina state finances escaped the prevailing financial chaos of the time. Tennessee continued state governmental operations long enough to legalize the issue of $3,000,000 in notes.[67]

Texas legislators also began to authorize the use of treasury warrants for current expenses in 1861, and these warrants were bringing less than fifty cents on the dollar in some sections of the state by April, 1861.[68] In November, the *State Gazette* reported a "general disposition to make treasury warrants receivable for State dues." On the strength of the "general disposition," holders of warrants were refusing to sell for less than par.[69] The Texas legislature in January, 1862, demanded specie for taxes levied for interest and principal payments on state loans. But treasury warrants were declared acceptable as payment for office fees, fees for patents, land dues, and all other dues collected by the state. An important exception in the 1862 law placed interest on school funds loaned to railroads within the category of taxes requiring specie payment.[70]

As Texas legislators convened in special meeting in May,

1864, a Texan predicted that the currency "embroglion [*sic*] will be the leading feature of the session."[71] He was not far wrong. Of the various remedies suggested to relieve currency depreciation, the legislature chose to order the comptroller to draw warrants on the treasurer to liquidate appropriations.[72] Furthermore, the governor was authorized to pay interest on the state's public debt in specie acquired from sale of state cotton. Any surplus specie could be used to redeem the treasury warrants, reserving always an amount necessary to purchase arms and ammunition for frontier defense.[73]

The attempts of the Texas legislature to restore waning confidence in the state's credit were not successful. The *Gazette* foresaw bankruptcy for Texas unless it resumed a specie basis, and the newspaper further expressed lack of faith in the effectiveness of any measure adopted by the general assembly.[74] H. R. Latimer wrote to the governor in November, 1864, that "The financial condition of the State & confederacy is indeed fearful, and the remedy beyond the control of Gov. or Legisl." He blamed speculation and the trade with Mexico for the state's ills, alleging that local prices had been shaped by the enormous charges on goods brought in from Mexico.[75]

The Virginia legislature approved the printing of treasury notes in the amount of $9,300,000 during 1861 and 1862.[76] By 1863 the currency of the state had come to "woeful depreciation."[77] A called session of the legislature meeting for six weeks in the fall of 1863 failed to pass remedial measures. But it also withheld authorization for new issues of notes; and the amount actually circulating remained for the rest of the war close to the $4,500,000 mark.[78]

In the search for revenue, Southern states approached tax increases with far more caution than they exhibited toward bonds and paper money. Florida retained its taxes throughout the war at the peace-time level.[79] In other states, tax increases were as a rule offset by generous extensions of time for payment.

The first substantial increase in Alabama taxes came in 1862 when the tax program raised levies on income from specified sources, such as medicine, dentistry, law and net profits from a great number of businesses, luxury items, and real estate.[80] The tax on real estate was twenty-five cents on each $100 of value. In 1863, Alabama adopted the policy of taxing state bonds and Confederate bonds, exempting the latter held by original purchasers from the Confederacy. The state taxed income from purchase and sale of money and credit instruments, levying a tax of seven and one-half per cent on the net profit from such transactions.[81] A blanket increase of thirty-three and one-third per cent was imposed in 1864 on all taxes set by earlier laws.[82]

The Arkansas convention had ordered one-third of the tax revenue paid in coin or overdue coupons. This stipulation met with repeal in 1861, and collection officials began to receive Confederate bonds or treasury notes and the bonds and warrants of the state for dues to the state.[83] The slight increase in taxes enacted in 1861 was repealed in December of the same year.[84] In 1862 the Arkansas general assembly suspended all laws for levy and collection of state taxes.[85] The Washington *Telegraph* feared the suspension law, considering it dangerously inflationary,[86] although county courts continued to levy taxes for various purposes: defense, relief and levee work.[87]

Georgia's tax law of 1861 gave the governor and comptroller general responsibility to set a rate that would provide a maximum of $1,000,000 in revenue.[88] The maximum was increased in 1862 to $1,500,000.[89] At the same session of the general assembly which set the latter figure, indigent relief drew an appropriation of $2,500,000 and soldiers' clothing, $1,500,000.[90] Obviously then, Georgia taxes were relatively insignificant in meeting the state's over-all budget for military and home-front needs.

A demand arose in Georgia for an income tax and for control of excess profits. The legislature in April, 1863, applied a graduated tax on income when profits amounted to twenty per cent on the certain investments.[91] The Savannah *Daily Morning News* printed an unsigned letter, allegedly written by G. B. Lamar, scoring the injustice of the bill's exemption of planters.[92] An income tax law which passed in the fall of 1863 began to tax profits over eight per cent on capital investment. This measure, unlike the earlier law, contained no specific exemption for agricultural producers.[93] And the 1865 income tax listed "persons engaged in agriculture and farming" among others subject to tax. The governor and comptroller were limited in setting tax rates to one per cent of the value of taxable property, as estimated in Confederate treasury notes.[94] The total receipts from ad valorem rate had been increased from $600,000 in 1861 to $1,500,000 in 1863.[95] The levy of twenty-five cents on the $100 in value, the rate for 1864, was still only one-fourth of the maximum permitted by the legislature at the time. In the 1864 tax law, which provided for the next year's revenue, the legislature reduced the maximum extent of taxation on property to one-half of one per cent.[96]

The Louisiana legislature provided for an ad valorem tax of one-sixth of one per cent on property, real and personal, on January 23, 1862, and on the same day postponed collection of state taxes by compulsory process.[97] Postponement was extended until 1865, with the exception of licenses on trades, professions or occupations.[98] Police juries, however, continued to levy and collect local taxes for "war purposes, support & subsistence of families of soldiers, [and] disabled soldiers. . . ."[99] In the last months of the war the legislature ordered collection in 1865 of back assessments for 1860, 1861, and 1864. Laws also raised the poll tax and license fees assessed under the act of March 15, 1855.[100]

The secession convention of Mississippi proposed to pay war expenses by a special tax of fifty per cent on the regular state tax and two-tenths of one per cent on money owned by citizens but deposited or used beyond state limits and on money withheld from circulation within the state.[101] To equip their own volunteers, counties could levy a special tax, the military relief tax, in an amount not to exceed 100 per cent of the state tax of 1861.[102] The legislature made an effort to increase taxable revenue by authorizing reports from county officials on land assessed at a value considered to be twenty per cent below the market value.[103]

Mississippi's tax laws of 1862 dealt largely with tax

relief. Military and levee taxes earlier imposed were suspended, and time limits for payment of taxes were extended.[104] The legislature enacted a law taxing sales, loans, and money on hand, and it raised the indigent relief tax to 150 per cent of the regular state tax.[105] In the last session of the Mississippi general assembly during the war, the legislators passed a tax-in-kind on producers of corn, wheat and bacon; a tax on profits of specified businesses; and a supplementary tax on property not subject to tax-in-kind.[106]

North Carolina enacted a measure in September, 1861, placing an ad valorem levy of one-fifth of one per cent on real and personal property. The act also taxed dividends, profits, and income from professions.[107] The convention in its third session included monies on hand and on deposit within the tax laws applying to land.[108] And the legislature meeting in the fall and winter of 1862-1863 raised the ad valorem to two-fifths of one per cent on real estate and many articles of personalty. A tax of two cents per dollar was placed on profits from manufacturing cotton, wool, leather, iron, tobacco, from steamboat corporations, and from purchase and sale of corn, flour, bacon, and provisions. The poll tax was raised to $1.20.[109] A member of the legislature wrote that the "revinew" bill was proving a "verry" troublesome thing and that taxes were bound to be "verry" high.[110] Again in 1864 taxes were raised, this time to one per cent on the ad valorem value. Other levies included a five per cent tax on profits in manufacture and trade.[111]

South Carolina's tax increase in 1861 was slight, raising tax revenue from $600,000 to about $800,000.[112] Even that increase met with some opposition. A diarist complained that the state had seceded to protect property and yet by the tax act had raised property taxes, leaving idle vagrants exempt from taxation.[113] No further revision of tax laws was made in 1862 and 1863, and South Carolina had a treasury balance of $800,000 at the end of 1862.[114] In 1864, however, almost every category of taxable property was affected by increased levies. The tax on every $100 of land jumped from $1.30, the rate for 1861 and 1862, to $6.00; income taxes for professional persons increased five-fold:

$1.00 per $100 to $5.00 per $100.[115] The legislature further established a tax-in-kind policy to accumulate stores needed for relief of the needy. The last increase in taxes occurred at the end of the war.[116]

Tennessee's tax laws in 1861 added fifteen cents to the already existing levy on every $100 of taxable property and assessed each corporation in the state an annual levy of $10.[117] Before time for another tax law, Tennessee's state government had disintegrated.

Agitation for an increase in Texas tax rates began in February, 1861, when a proposal for a tax of two-fifths of one per cent on every $100 was rejected by the legislature.[118] The governor, Edward Clark, approved an increase of the direct tax from twelve to twenty cents on $100.[119] His general assembly was content to tax money lent at interest or used for buying or selling exchange or other currency at twenty cents on each $100. The legislature also taxed sales of goods, wares, merchandise and liquors twenty cents on $100 value.[120] The next legislature went even beyond Clark's recommendation and set a rate of twenty-five cents on every $100 of real and personal property, and levied a poll tax of $1.00. It also raised license fees on many professions and enterprises.[121]

The *Tri-Weekly Telegraph* in 1863 suggested taxation "up to the eyes, when the debt is accumulating, and when we are able to pay it, rather than defer it to such a time as we shall have less currency than we want, and hard times shall be upon us."[122] The legislature in March of this year doubled the ad valorem tax and the tax on money lent or securities dealt in.[123]

Virginia's tax revenue amounted to about $2,000,000 in 1861.[124] Tax revisions were adopted by the legislature in April, 1861; the new law set a forty cent rate on $100 of real and personal property and provided for an income tax of one per cent over the $500 exemption.[125] Increases in 1862 brought rates of sixty cents for every $100 ad valorem and further hikes in rates on money loaned, interest received, incomes, and licenses.[126] The Richmond *Enquirer* on January 3, 1863, urged higher taxes to provide for a sinking fund for debts, arguing against the wisdom of borrowing to pay interest on previous loans.[127] Instead, the legislature repealed rate increases in 1863 and lowered taxes in 1864.[128] It is interesting that the *Enquirer,* having espoused the cause of high taxes in 1863, approved tax relief in 1864. As justification for lowered taxes this newspaper in February, 1864, called attention to the treasury surplus, the premiums which state bonds carried, the dividends on Virginia Improvements shares, and the demand for Virginia treasury notes.[129]

Exemption or moratoriums on payment of taxes tended to undo the benefits that might have arisen from such tax increases as Southern state legislatures would permit. Property damaged or destroyed in invaded areas brought lower assessment evaluations. Tax collecting everywhere was complicated by changes in laws, absence of regular officials due to military service, and incompetency or neglect on the part of their replacements.[130]

Some states sought to conserve funds by retrenchment, by consolidation of offices, or by eliminating dispensable positions. A Georgia bill for reduction of the salaries of the governor, supreme court judges, and members of the legislature passed over the governor's veto.[131] The governor's request in 1862 for a fifty per cent increase in salaries to meet mounting living costs was unavailing.[132]

As time went on, conditions forced several states to increase salaries.[133] Those states which authorized no increases provided some additional compensation in the form of substantial rental allowances for state officials. Louisiana did not raise the governor's salary from the $4000 figure of 1861, but by 1865 the state was appropriating $3000 for the chief executive's rent and $1000 each for rent for the secretary of state, the treasurer, and the auditor.[134] South Carolina gave its governor $1200 annually for the same purpose.[135] The legislature of North Carolina, on the other hand, not only made a sizeable increase in the salary of its governor, but also allowed him in 1863 to draw $500 of his salary from the state funds held by financial agents in foreign countries.[136] To offset rising costs, unnecessary state offices were at times eliminated in the interest of economy. Louisiana abolished the offices of state engineer and state librarian.[137] Georgia consolidated the offices of secretary of state and surveyor general.[138] And South Carolina abolished the position of paymaster of state troops.[139]

Nevertheless, despite all revenue expedients, Southern states were on the verge of financial chaos in the last winter of the war. Louisiana was finding a partial solution for her money problems in 1865 and South Carolina's State Bank kept her economy reasonably stable. But even in those states and to a greater degree elsewhere in the South a breakdown of credit and money necessitated a return to barter system of exchange. Prices of commodities rose faster than state legislatures could print their lavish issues of paper. Every Confederate defeat or stale-mate affected the value of state bonds. Furthermore, state authorities found it well-nigh impossible to collect taxes. By early spring of 1865 there were few thoughtful Southerners who failed to see that the collapse of Southern economy presaged defeat of the Southern cause.

★

VIII

THE END OF THE EXPERIMENT

As HE SURVEYED the prevailing scarcity and want in 1863, a Mississippian made the gloomy prediction: "It would paralize [sic] the efforts of the Army to know that their homes are the scenes of want and almost starvation."[1] The prediction seemed fulfilled in 1863 when the Confederate army began "visibly melting away."[2] At the end of the war deserters numbered about 100,000 out of a white population of less than 6,000,000. Alabama, Mississippi, and North Carolina had extensive areas of "deserter-country."[3] And all over the South the presence of service men absent without leave complicated an already snarled social and economic order and contributed profoundly to the loss of the will to fight.

Desertion was not the sole evidence of the collapse of the Confederacy. Trading with the enemy became flagrant in sections near the federal lines; everywhere Union sympathizers and activities increased; and the expediency of peace moves occupied many hours in legislative sessions.

The Nashville *Patriot* had made a shrewd prognostication about trade with the North months before the war began.

We would be glad, to see Tennessee and all other Southern States supply their own wants and wants of one another, but they can't do it just yet. . . . Besides, people will buy where they can get the best bargains, whether that be as far North as Nova Scotia, or as far South as the Equinoctial line.[4]

In the South, trading with Northern merchants was more than bargain-hunting; it was a desperation measure to obtain supplies for home wants and for military needs. Both Confederate and Union agents gave unofficial sanction to trade between the lines.[5] State governors and legislatures did little to control the traffic. Instead, they sometimes encouraged it and occasionally participated in it. General Gideon Pillow, commanding the Army of Tennessee, opposed trade through the Memphis blockade in May, 1861. When the governor of Tennessee at the request of the governor of Louisiana permitted the steamer *Louisville* to pass with her cargo, Pillow felt that such exceptions would lead to a general flouting of trade restrictions. "There are strong manifestations of mob violence here this evening at my order allowing the *Louisville* to go forward," he reported.[6]

Several state legislatures outlawed traffic with the enemy early in the war.[7] Governor John Milton of Florida made repeated efforts to obtain laws prohibiting the trade.[8] But whether or not control legislation existed, the traffic continued. A Georgian wrote his governor in March, 1862, that Union men in McMinn County, Tennessee, were buying cotton with Confederate paper and taking it into Tennessee for storage.[9] J. Addison Denny informed the governor of Texas in 1862 that cotton destined supposedly for Mexico was being routed to the North from Brownsville.[10] From 1862 through 1865 goods flowed freely from the North into the Federal occupied Southern areas and less openly across the lines. Professor Ramsdell tells of poor families near Federal lines who organized wagon trains to carry cotton to the Federals and to bring back supplies.[11] Planters in some areas followed their example. James Lusk Alcorn, brigadier general of Mississippi troops, described his own trading operations in letters to his wife and scornfully named former ardent secessionists who furtively sought greenbacks and provisions in exchange for their Delta cotton.[12]

Governor Charles Clark of Mississippi made favorable contracts for cotton and woolen cards with private companies, which he knew to be engaged in shipping cotton to New Orleans and Memphis.[13] Governor Clark reported to the legislature that acting under authority of an 1863 law which had ordered him to purchase supplies wherever they might be obtained he had attempted to secure presidential approval for the trade but without success.[14] The general assembly meeting in March of 1865 disavowed any intention of sanctioning trade between the lines in the act of 1863 and repealed it.[15] Memphis, Vicksburg, and New Orleans in the Mississippi Valley were centers of brisk extra-legal trade; other areas as well were affected by trade with the enemy.[16] The policy of Confederate officials toward the problem was vacillating. Army officers were inclined to approve illegal trade to obtain stores for their men; civil officials often were willing to permit the trade to relieve distress among the poor.[17]

Desertions and commercial intercourse with the enemy gave heart to the Southern Unionists whom the fierce emotionalism of secessionists had but temporarily quieted in 1861. Many Unionists and cooperationists had felt betrayed by their own delegates in secession conventions.[18] Others had accepted secession in the vain hope that a subsequent appeal to the people would lead to a defeat of the disunionists.[19] Some never acquiesced.[20] When the conditions of war brought hardships to Southern people and Confederate policies evoked dissatisfaction among states' leaders, unionism emerged as a powerful, disruptive force in the South. It drew strength from the decline of Confederate military prospects in the West in 1862 and 1863 and from the stalemate in the East from 1863 to 1865.[21] Louisiana felt the sting of Unionist activities after the fall of New Orleans.[22] Disloyal elements in Alabama and Mississippi received encouragement from the Federals in occupation of Tennessee. Even in Texas, little affected by military operations, the growth of anti-Confederate sentiment was consistent during the war.[23]

The first organized movement for peace was the Peace and Constitutional Society formed in Van Buren County, Arkansas, 1861.[24] The Houston *Tri-Weekly Telegraph* announced a secret "abolition society" in North Texas with members in several Texas militia companies. The society reputedly had a "grip, a sign, a password" and constituted a spy system for the Federals.[25]

Alabama's Unionists were active as early as 1861. Indeed, in November, 1862, a member of the Alabama legislature was expelled for "complicity with the enemy."[26] By 1862, Huntsville had become notorious for its treason; and many prominent citizens were implicated throughout North Alabama.[27] A Virginian expressed concern in 1863 over an Alabama organization called the Washington Constitutional Union.[28] John Clisby, writing to Governor Shorter in that year, said that the movement was "open, bold and defiant. . . . The earnest desire is not for independence but reunion."[29]

The various dissident movements apparently coalesced to a degree when the Peace Society came into existence. The Peace Society drew members from Mississippi, Alabama, East Tennessee, and Georgia.[30] In North Carolina the "Red Strings," or the Order of the Heroes of America, came into being. Its influence reached across the border into South Carolina and Southwest Virginia.[31]

Deserters, stragglers, and Unionists possessed a natural affinity for peace societies, but peace moves and reconstructionist agitation were by no means confined to them. Rumors of reconstruction in the North Carolina legislature in 1863 prompted the introduction and passage of a Senate resolution denouncing the accusation and avowing loyalty to the Confederacy. In the fall of 1863, after the Congressional elections, resolutions asking that the Confederate president begin negotiations looking toward peace failed of passage. By 1864, however, majority opinion in the North Carolina general assembly had reversed this position and resolved: "It becomes our government, through its appropriate constitutional department to use its earnest efforts to put an end to this unnatural and unChristian work of carnage." The resolution suggested that a peace proposal should follow a signal military victory on the part of the South, lest the action be imputed to fear of defeat.

When the North Carolina legislature met in regular session in 1864, a select joint committee recommended passage of resolutions providing for an "honorable" peace. The committee held that since the United States government had refused to recognize Confederate commissioners because of implied recognition of the Confederate government, the Federal administration might well receive commissioners representing the states. It suggested the appointment of such commissioners to receive their orders and powers from the president of the Confederate and not from the state governments. Although the resolutions did not pass, their appearance occasioned much comment. One Texas newspaper said that "Old Rip Vanwinkle must behave better than that . . . else we are a ruined people."

In Georgia the year 1864 brought the question of reconstruction to the fore in legislative sessions. A message of Governor Brown to this general assembly in April denounced the Confederate administration and urged consideration of peace overtures by the "people of the South.[37] The message led a Florida newspaper to draw the conclusion that rebel politicians were losing faith in their chances of winning the war.[38] Meantime, Linton Stephens had introduced resolutions in the special session of the legislature suggesting that the Confederate government make an offer of peace with a proviso permitting border states to settle their destiny by conventions elected after removal of all military forces.[39] Linton Stephens' resolution in November, 1864, was stronger. Both the governor and Stephens took the position that the states should call a convention to consider peace.[40] The general assembly did not concur, and in February of the next year another resolution for a peace convention failed to obtain majority approval. The *Countryman* noted the fact that many reconstructionists of 1865 were fire-eaters of 1861.[41]

The Memphis *Daily Appeal* in 1864 reported that the Alabama legislature had entertained several proposals for peace, none of which had passed. The peace propositions made in Alabama, however, had independence not reconstruction as the condition.[42]

William W. Boyce, a Confederate Congressman, assumed leadership of peace forces in the South Carolina legislature in 1863.[43] The South Carolina General Assembly continued to shun peace moves, and the re-election of Lincoln confirmed the majority of South Carolina legislators in that position. The general assembly declared that a convention of states would be "unconstitutional and dangerous."[44]

Talk of peace with victory or a negotiated peace based on independence was sheer sophistry after Sherman's march and the surrender of the Army of Northern Virginia. And Lincoln's assassination frustrated the chance of a mild reconstruction policy.

Thus ended the Southern experiment. With slim resources of money and credit, and of industrial productivity, the South attempted to sustain political theories of particularism at a time when its economy was closely interwoven with that of the Union. The South began the fight for the particularism it espoused armed with little more than constitutional principles. State governments rushed into the breach left by a withdrawal of Northern money, credit, and goods. They devised paper schemes to support local and Confederate defense, to maintain business-as-usual economy and normalcy in the operation of social and political institutions. They set up relief programs. They squared shoulders under burdersome responsibilities to their people and to their nation. But a pervading weakness sapped at a foundation of Southern society. With little money, dwindling credit, and inadequate industrial productivity Southern states could build only with straw. They could not set the house in order and they could not prevent its collapse.

★

NOTES

CHAPTER I

1. *Journal of the Mississippi Convention . . . 1861 . . .* (Jackson 1861), pp. 87-88; *Journal of the Convention of . . . South Carolina, 1860, 1861 and 1862 . . .* (Columbia, 1862), pp. 325-331, 461-466; *Journal of the . . . Convention . . . of Florida, 1861* (Tallahassee, 1861), pp. 25-26, 31-32; *Ordinances and Constitution of the State of Alabama. . . .* (Montgomery, 1861), pp. 3-4; *Journal . . . of the Convention of . . . Georgia, . . .* (Milledgeville, 1861), pp. 104-113; *Journal of . . . the Louisiana State Convention, . . .* (New Orleans, 1861), pp. 13-14; Earnest William Winkler, ed., *Journal of the Secession Convention of Texas, 1861. . . .* (Austin, 1912), pp. 18-21. Citation of laws, journals, and other official documents will be condensed throughout the notes.

2. J. G. Randall, *The Civil War and Reconstruction* (Boston, 1937), pp 245-248.

3. *Ordinances of the Arkansas Convention . . . 1861* (Little Rock, 1861), pp. 3-6, 88; *Ordinances . . . of the Convention of Virginia, . . . in April, May, June and July, 1861* (Richmond, 1861), p. 3; James Welch Patton, *Unionism and Reconstruction in Tennessee 1860-1869* (Chapel Hill, 1934), p. 21; *Journal of the Convention . . . of North Carolina, . . . 1861* (Raleigh, 1862), p. 13.

4. *Journal of the Louisiana Conven-*

tion (1861), pp. 235-236; 251-252, 255.

5. *Constitution of Texas as Amended in 1861 . . . Ordinances of the Texas Convention* (Austin, 1861), pp. 38-39.

6. *Ordinances and Constitution of Alabama* (1861), pp. 54-71; *Acts and Resolutions . . . General Assembly of Florida . . . 1860* (Tallahassee, 1861), p. 234; *Ibid., 1862* (Tallahassee, 1863), pp. 57-58; *Acts of the General Assembly of Arkansas, . . .* [1862] (Washington, 1896), pp. 31-32; *Laws of the State of Mississippi, 1861, 1862* (Jackson, 1862), pp. 277-278; *Journal of the Louisiana Convention* (1861), pp. 263-265; *Ordinances of the Texas Convention* (1861), p. 28.

7. *General Laws of Texas* [1861-1862] (Houston, 1862), pp. 21-22; *Ordinances of the Arkansas Convention* (May Session, 1861), pp. 53-55; *Acts of the Florida General Assembly* (Twelfth, First Session, 1862), pp. 39-42.

8. H. S. Bradford to Governor Isham G. Harris, July 12, 1861, in Governors' Papers, Tennessee State Library.

9. *Journal of the South Carolina Convention* (1860-1861, and 1862 Sessions), pp. 758-759.

10. *Journal of the Florida Convention* January Session, 1861), p. 63, 103; *Journal of the Georgia Convention* (1861), p. 375; *Journal of the Louisiana Convention* (1861), pp. 235-237; *Journal of the Mississippi Conven-*

tion (January Session, 1861), p. 143; *Journal of the South Carolina Convention* (1860, 1861, and 1862 Sessions), pp. 758-759; David Y. Thomas, *Arkansas in War and Reconstruction, 1861-1874* (Little Rock, 1926), p. 86; John K. Bettersworth, *Confederate Mississippi, The People and Policies of a Cotton State in Wartime* (Baton Rouge, 1943), p. 11.

11. *Acts of the Second Called Session, 1861, and of the First Regular Annual Session of the General Assembly of Alabama,* . . . (Montgomery, 1862), p. 49; *Acts of the Florida General Assembly* (Tenth Session, 1860), pp. 241-242; T. Conn Bryan, *Confederate Georgia* (Athens, 1953), p. 13; *Acts of Louisiana, in Extra Session . . . December, 1862, & January, 1863* (Natchitoches, 1864), p. 32; *Journal of the South Carolina Convention* (1860, 1861, and 1862 Sessions), pp. 768-769; *Acts of Virginia, Extra Session, 1862,* . . . (Richmond, 1862), p. 104.

12. Lillian A. Hamrick, ed., *A Guide to the Microfilm Collection of Early State Records* . . . (Library of Congress, 1950-51), p. 257, identifies these three sessions as follows: January 20-February 6, adjourned session; April 3-10 and September 21-30, called sessions. The regular session met from November 23 through December 17.

13. Washington (Arkansas) *Telegraph,* August 6, 1862.

14. Austin (Texas) *State Gazette,* November 2, 1861.

15. T. J. McClellan to Bess, November 14, 1861, in Buchanan-McClellan Papers, Southern Historical Collection, University of North Carolina.

16. Raleigh *Standard,* December 24, 1862.

17. Nashville *Patriot,* November 2, 1861.

18. New Orleans *Daily Crescent,* December 21, 1861.

19. Edward Younger, ed., *Inside the Confederate Government. The Diary of Robert Garlick Hill Kean* (New York, 1957), p. 22.

20. Mary C. Simms Oliphant, Alfred Taylor Odell, T. C. Duncan Eaves, eds., *The Letters of William Gilmore Simms* (Columbia, 1956), IV, 417.

21. Unsigned letter to "Dear Gourdin," December 10, 1861, in Gourdin-Young Letters, Emory University Library.

22. Selma *Morning Reporter,* November 1, 1862, quoting the Montgomery *Mail.*

23. Joseph D. Shields to his wife, no date, in Shields Papers, 1802-1927, in Department of Archives and Manuscripts, Louisiana State University.

24. Austin *State Gazette,* November 9, November 23, 1861.

25. Tallahassee *Florida Sentinel,* December 9, 1862.

26. *Ibid.,* November 10, 1863.

27. Raleigh *State Journal,* September 25, 1861.

28. L. Sharpe to his wife, November 29, 1862, in Sharpe Papers, Southern Historical Collection, University of North Carolina.

29. Montgomery *Mail,* August 5, 1863.

30. C. C. Clay, Jr., to Louis T. Wigfall, September 11, 1863, in C. C. Clay, Jr. Papers, Library of Congress.

31. Milledgeville *Southern Federal Union,* December 24, 1861.

32. Turnwold (Georgia) *Countryman,* March 28, 1865.

33. Raleigh *Semi-Weekly Register,* June 14, 1862.

34. Raleigh *Weekly Standard,* August 20, 1862.

35. Wilmington *Journal,* January 14, 1863.

36. Anonymous, *The Great Panic: Being Incidents Connected with Two Weeks of the War in Tennessee. By an Eye-Witness* (Nashville, 1862), pp. 10-11.

37. Richmond *Daily Examiner,* May 15, 1862.

38. Diary of Anna Green, November 19, 1864, p. 91, in possession of William L. Proctor, Chicago, Illinois.

39. Harris County (Georgia) *Enterprise*, November 25, 1864.

40. *Journal of the Mississippi Convention March, 1861* (Jackson, 1861), pp. 79-80.

41. *Ordinances and Constitution of Alabama* (1861), p. 53.

42. *Journal of the Georgia Convention* (1861), p. 391.

43. *Report of the Committee on Public Safety to the Convention of the . . . State of Texas, . . .* (Austin, 1861), pp. 5-11.

44. Lane Carter Kendall, "The Interregnum in Louisiana in 1861. The Course of Events in the State from November, 1860, to April, 1861," *Louisiana Historical Quarterly*, XVI (April, 1933), 177.

45. New Orleans *Daily True Delta*, February 9, 1861.

46. Baton Rouge *Daily Advocate*, March 21, 1861.

47. William Lamar Gammon II, "Governor John Milton of Florida, Confederate States of America," unpublished M.A. Thesis, University of Florida, 1948, p. 141.

48. Tallahassee *Florida Sentinel*, January 14, 1862.

49. John Milton to C. H. Austin, February 22, 1862, in Governor John Milton Letter Book, 1861-1863, Florida Historical Society Library. Hereafter cited as Milton Letter Book, 1861-1863.

50. Richmond *Examiner*, April 12, 1861.

51. Joseph M. Stevens to Mary Jane Harrison, April 6, 1861, in Tucker-Harrison-Smith Papers, University of Virginia Library.

52. Richmond *Examiner*, April 29, June 13, June 19, December 2, 1861.

53. Lowry Price Ware, "The South Carolina Executive Councils of 1861 and 1862," unpublished M.A. Thesis, University of South Carolina, 1952, p. 29.

54. Charles Edward Cauthen, *South Carolina Goes to War 1860-1865* (Chapel Hill, 1950), p. 143.

55. David Flavel Jamison to Governor F. W. Pickens, March 5, 1862, in F. W. Pickens Papers, Duke University Library.

56. Cauthen, pp. 142-153, 159-161 .

57. J. G. de Roulhac Hamilton, *North Carolina Since 1860* (Chicago, 1919), p. 5.

58. J. G. de Roulhac Hamilton, ed., *The Correspondence of Jonathan Worth* (Raleigh, 1909), X, 153-154, 159, 167-169.

59. Raleigh *Standard*, June 22, July 10, September 21, 1861.

60. Wilmington *Daily Journal*, June 14, 1861.

61. Aubrey Lee Brooks and Hugh Talmage Lefler, eds., *The Papers of Walter Clark* (Chapel Hill, 1948), I, 60.

62. Hillsborough (North Carolina) *Recorder*, May 14, 1862, quoting William Alexander Graham.

63. Zebulon B. Vance to Weldon N. Edwards, September 18, 1862, in Governor Zebulon B. Vance Letter Book, 1862-1863, North Carolina Department of Archives and History. Hereafter cited as Vance Letter Book, 1862-1863.

64. Raleigh *Semi-Weekly Register*, October 25, 1862.

CHAPTER II

1. Frank Lawrence Owsley, "Local Defense and the Overthrow of the Confederacy: A Study in States Rights," *Mississippi Valley Historical Review* XI (1925), 490-525.

2 Cauthen, p. 115.

3. Bettersworth, p. 28.

4. *Ordinances and Constitution of Alabama* (1861), pp. 9-13.

5. *Acts of . . . the State of Georgia . . ., November and December, 1860* (Milledgeville, 1861), pp. 50-52.

6. Douglas Southall Freeman, *R. E. Lee: A Biography* (New York, 1948), I, 493.

7. *Public Laws of the State of North Carolina . . . First Extra Session of 1861* (Raleigh, 1861), pp. 95-98.

8. *Journal of the North Carolina Convention* (First Session, 1861), pp. 8-10; Raleigh *Standard,* August 24, 1861.

9. *Public Laws of the State of North Carolina . . . Second Extra Session of 1861* (Raleigh, 1861), pp. 52-53.

10. *Public Acts of the State of Tennessee . . . [Second] Extra Session . . .* April, 1861 (Nashville, 1861), pp. 21-32.

11. *Ordinances of the Texas Convention* (1861), pp. 33-34; *General Laws of the Texas Legislature,* 1861-62, pp. 8-10.

12. *Journal of the House of Representatives of the State of South Carolina: . . .* 1862 (Columbia, 1863), p. 5.

13 Bettersworth, pp. 56, 71-72.

14. William Watson Davis, *The Civil War and Reconstruction in Florida* (New York, 1913), pp. 143-144.

15. *Acts of the Louisiana Legislature* (Extra Session, 1862-63), pp. 18-20.

16. *Acts of the Virginia General Assembly* (Extra Session, 1862), pp. 8-9; *Acts of the State of Virginia, . . . Adjourned Session,* 1863, . . . Richmond, 1863), pp. 39-41.

17. Raleigh *Register,* January 3, 1863; Wilmington *Journal,* January 1, 1863.

18. *Public Laws of the North Carolina General Assembly* (Second Extra Session, 1861), pp. 18-46. For an account of the militia in action, see John G. Barrett, *The Civil War in North Carolina* (Chapel Hill, 1963), pp. 100-102.

19. *Acts of . . . the State of South Carolina, December, 1861* (Columbia, 1862), pp. 11-14.

20. *Acts of the Alabama General Assembly* (Second Called and Regular Sessions, 1861), pp. 86-87; *General Laws of the Texas Legislature* (Regular Session, 1861), pp. 11-21.

21. *Acts of the General Assembly of*

the *State of Virginia, Passed in 1861-2,* . . . (Richmond, 1862), pp. 4-8.

22. *Laws of the Mississippi Legislature,* (1861-62), pp. 193-195.

23. Bettersworth, p. 47.

24. *Acts . . . of the State of Louisiana, . . ., 1861* (Baton Rouge, 1862), pp. 61-62.

25. *Public Acts of the State of Tennessee, . . . First Session . . . 1861* (Nashville, 1862), pp. 20-26.

26. Davis, p. 88.

27. *Journal . . . of the House of Representatives . . . State of Florida . . ., 1860* (Tallahassee, 1861), pp. 251-255; *Journal . . . of the Senate . . . of Florida . . ., 1862* (Tallahassee, 1862), pp. 25-63; *Ibid., 1863* [Second Session] (Tallahassee, 1863), pp. 69-71.

28. John Milton to George W. Randolph, August 5, 1862, in Milton Letter Book.

29. Turnwold *Countryman,* March 4, 1862; *Journal of the . . . State of Georgia . . . 1862* (Milledgeville, 1862), pp. 26-27.

30. Washington *Telegraph,* April 3, 1862.

31. *Battles and Leaders of the Civil War . . .* (New York, 1887-1898), III, Pt. II, 443.

32. Richmond *Examiner,* February 8, 1862.

33. R. C. Parker to Governor John Gills Shorter, February 25, 1862, in Governors' Papers, Alabama Department of Archives and History.

34. Cauthen, p. 146.

35. *Acts of the General Assembly of . . . South Carolina, September and December, 1863* (Columbia, 1864), pp. 171-173.

36. *Acts of the General Assembly . . . of South Carolina, 1864-65* (Columbia, 1866), p. 249.

37. *Laws of the State of Mississippi Passed . . ., Dec. 1862 and Nov. 1863* (Selma, Alabama, 1864), pp. 101-108; *Laws of the State of Mis-*

sissippi . . . Called Session . . .,
August 1864 (Meridian, Mississippi,
1864), pp. 16-18.

38. Walter L. Fleming, Civil War and
Reconstruction in Alabama (Cleveland, 1911), p. 89.

39. Petition to Governor John Gill
Shorter, March 3, 1862; James Montgomery to Governor Shorter, April
5, 1862; James M. Pearson to Governor Shorter, April 12, 1862, in
Governors' Papers.

40. Fleming, pp. 90-91.

41. General Laws of the Extra Session
. . . of the State of Texas [1863]
(Austin, 1863), pp. 32-33.

42. John Q. Anderson, ed., Brokenburn,
The Journal of Kate Stone 1861-
1868 (Baton Rouge, 1955), p. 229.

43. General Laws . . . of the State of
Texas [1863] (Houston, 1864), pp.
44-45.

44. Houston Daily Telegraph, February
8, 1864.

45. Public Laws of the State of North
Carolina . . . Adjourned Session,
1862-63 (Raleigh, 1863), pp. 16-18.

46. Public Laws of the State of North
Carolina . . . Called Session, 1863
(Raleigh, 1863), pp. 8-10; Barrett,
p. 20.

47. Acts of the Louisiana Legislature
(Extra Session, 1862-63), pp. 36-40.

48. Charles le D. Elgee to Governor
Thomas O. Moore, May 1, 1863, in
Thomas O. Moore Papers, Louisiana
State University Department of
Archives and History.

49. Journal of the House of Representatives . . . of Louisiana . . . First
Session . . ., 1864 (Shreveport, 1864),
p. 31. Jefferson Davis Bragg, Louisiana in the Confederacy (Baton
Rouge, 1943), pp. 162-163.

50. Acts of the General Assembly of
. . . Georgia, . . ., November and
December, 1863; Also Extra Session
of 1864 (Milledgeville, 1864), pp.
51-58.

51. Journal of the House of Represen-

tatives of . . . Georgia . . ., 1864
(Milledgeville, 1864), pp. 122-123.

52. John Milton to General Richard F.
Floyd, January 29, 1863, in Milton
Letter Book.

53. Acts and Resolutions Adopted by
the General Assembly of Florida . . .
1864 (Tallahassee, 1865), pp. 10-13.

54. Governor's Message to the General
Assembly, Virginia, January 25,
1864, in Executive Papers, Virginia
State Library.

55. Richmond Enquirer, January 29,
February 12, 1864.

56. Acts of the South Carolina General
Assembly (1861), pp. 11-14; Laws of
the Mississippi Legislature (1861-
62), pp. 193-196; Acts of the Called
Session of the General Assembly of
Alabama, . . . January, 1861 (Mont-
gomery, 1861), p. 55; Acts of the
Alabama General Assembly (Second
Called and Regular Sessions, 1861),
p. 73; Acts of the Called Session,
1862, and of the Second Annual
Session of the General Assembly of
Alabama, . . . 1862 (Montgomery,
1863), p. 64; Acts of the Louisiana
Legislature (First Session, 1861), pp.
61-72; Acts of the Virginia General
Assembly (Extra Session, 1862), pp.
149-151.

57. Acts of the Called Session, 1863,
and of the Third Annual Session of
the General Assembly of Alabama,
. . . 1863 (Montgomery, 1863), pp.
96-97; Acts of the Louisiana Legislature (Extra Session, 1862-63), pp.
36-40; Acts . . . of the State of
Louisiana, . . . Extra Session . . .,
1863 (Shreveport, 1863), pp. 42-48;
Laws of the Mississippi Legislature
(Called Session, 1862; Regular Session, 1863), pp. 101-106; Public
Laws of the North Carolina General Assembly (Adjourned Session,
1862-63), pp. 16-18; Laws of the
Mississippi Legislature (Called Session, August, 1964), pp. 16-18; Acts
of the South Carolina General As-

sembly (September and December Sessions, 1863), pp. 188-190.

58. *Journal of the Senate of . . . Mississippi, Called Session, at Macon, August, 1864* (Meridian, 1864), pp. 83-84; Governor's Message to the General Assembly, Virginia, March 25, 1862, Executive Papers, Virginia State Library.

59. Edward Callohill Burks to Rowland D. Buford, January 20, 1861, in Edward Callohill Burks Letters, University of Virginia Library.

60. *Acts of the General Assembly of . . . South Carolina . . . November and December, 1860, and January, 1861* (Columbia, 1861), pp. 356-58; *Acts of the General Assembly of . . . Virginia, . . . Extra Session, 1861, . . .* (Richmond, 1861), pp. 27-28.

61. *Report of the Committee on Public Safety to the Texas Convention* (1861), pp. 5-11.

62. *Journal of the Mississippi Convention* (January Session, 1861), p. 64; *Laws of the State of Mississippi . . . January 1861* (Jackson, 1861), p. 37; *Laws of the Mississippi Legislature* (1861-62), p. 67; *Public Laws of the State of North Carolina, 1860-61; . . .* (Raleigh, 1861), pp. 53-54; *Public Acts of the Tennessee General Assembly* (Second Extra Session, 1861), pp. 49-50; *Public Acts of the Tennessee General Assembly* (First Session, 1861-62), pp. 65-71; Bragg, p. 52.

63. United States War Department, comp., *The War of the Rebellion; . . .* (Washington, 1880-1901), series IV, I, pp. 404-405, 422, 582, 575-76, 658. Hereafter cited as *O.R.*

64. W. W. Harllee and W. H. Gist to James M. Shackelford, March 17, 1862, in Executive Papers, South Carolina Department of Archives and History. Hereafter cited as Executive Papers, South Carolina.

65. W. G. Eason to Governor F. W. Pickens, November 5, 1862, in Legislative Papers, South Carolina Department of Archives and History. Hereafter cited as Legislative Papers, South Carolina.

66. *Acts of the Virginia General Assembly* (1861-62), pp. 55-56, *Laws of the Mississippi Legislature* (1861-62), pp. 232-34; *Public Acts of the Tennessee General Assembly* (First Session, 1861-62), p. 30.

67. Thomas, p. 102; Bettersworth, p. 23; Governor Edward Clark to Thomas P. Carothers, August 29, 1861, in Executive Record Book, no. 80, Texas State Library.

68. Governor F. R. Lubbock to Col. James I. Cook, January 3, 1862, in Executive Record Book, no. 81, Texas State Library, Austin. Hereafter cited as Executive Record Book, no. 81, Texas.

69. *General Laws of the Texas Legislature* (1861-62), pp. 40-41.

70. Annie Cowling, "The Civil War Trade of the Lower Rio Grande Valley," unpublished M.A. Thesis, University of Texas, 1926, pp. 62-63.

71. James Arthur Irby, "Confederate Austin 1861-1865," unpublished M.A. Thesis, University of Texas, 1953, pp. 68-69.

72. *General Laws of the Texas Legislature* (1863), p. 25.

73. *Public Laws of the North Carolina Assembly* (Second Extra Session, 1861), p. 4; *Private Laws of the State of North Carolina . . . Second Extra Session, 1861* (Raleigh, 1861), p. 92.

74. Daniel Harvey Hill, *Bethel to Sharpsburg, A History of North Carolina in the War between the States* (Raleigh, 1926), I, 333-34.

75. *Public Laws of the State of North Carolina . . . Adjourned Session, 1863* (Raleigh, 1863), p. 28.

76. *Ibid.*, 1864 (Raleigh, 1864), pp. 22-23.

77. J. G. de Roulac Hamilton, *The Correspondence of Jonathan Worth*, I, 274-275.

78. *Acts of the Georgia General Assem-*

bly (1863; Extra Session, 1864), pp. 9-10.

79. Bryan, p. 94.

80. Edwin B. Coddington, "The Activities and Attitudes of a Confederate Business Man: Gazaway B. Lamar," *Journal of Southern History* IX (1943), 3-36.

CHAPTER III

1. C. C. S. Farrar, *The War, Its Causes and Consequences* (Memphis, 1864), p. 191.

2. *O. R.*, series IV, I, 117, 126-127.

3 *Ibid.*, pp. 129-132, 149,150, 176, 174; series I, I, 298. *Journal of the Mississippi Convention* (March Session, 1861), pp. 94-95; *Acts of the State of Louisiana . . . January, 1861* (Baton Rouge, 1861), p. 113; *Ordinances of the Arkansas Convention* (May Session, 1861), pp. 7-8; *Ordinances of the Virginia Convention* (April-July Session, 1861), p. 49; *Public Laws of the North Carolina General Assembly* (Second Extra Session, 1861), p. 15; *Public Acts of the Tennessee General Assembly (Extra Session, 1861)*, p. 75.

4. *O. R.*, series IV, I, 181, 206, 214.

5. E. Merton Coulter, *The Confederate States of America 1861-65*, vol. VII in *A History of the South* (Baton Rouge, 1950), p. 308.

6. *Acts and Resolutions the General Assembly of Florida . . . , 1861* (Tallahassee, 1862), p. 74.

7. *O. R.*, series IV, I, 366.

8. *Public Laws of the North Carolina General Assembly* (Second Extra Session, 1861), p. 122.

9. *O. R.*, series IV, I, 316-317, 302, 348-350.

10. *Laws of the State of Mississippi . . . Called Session . . . July, 1861* (Jackson, 1861), pp. 45-46.

11. *Journal of the Convention of North Carolina, . . . January and February, 1862* (Raleigh, 1862), p. 113; *Acts of the Virginia General Assembly* (1861-62), p. 143.

12. Richmond *Dispatch,* May 8, 1862; *Journal of the Florida Senate* (First Session, 1862), pp. 25-63; *Selma Morning Reporter,* October 30, 1862.

13. Turnwold, *Countryman,* "Letter from Mrs. Poke," November 24, 1862.

14. James Chesnut, Jr. to Adjutant Inspector General of South Carolina, May 10, 1862, in Chesnut-Manning-Miller Papers, South Carolina Historical Society. Microfilm in Eugene C. Barker Library, University of Texas.

15. John B. Galbraith to Governor John Milton, April 28, 1862, in Manuscript Opinions of the Attorney-General, Florida, January 3, 1850-May 22, 1866, Florida State Library.

16. Jackson *Weekly Mississippian,* November 20, 1862.

17. Montgomery *Mail,* November 29, 1862.

18. *Public Laws of the State of North Carolina . . . 1862-63; . . .* (Raleigh, 1863), pp. 49-50.

19. *General Laws . . . (Called Session) . . . of the State of Texas* (Houston, 1864), p. 17.

20. *Public Laws of the North Carolina General Assembly* (Adjourned Session, 1864), p. 26; *Acts of the General Assembly of . . . Virginia . . . 1863-64, . . .* (Richmond, 1864), pp. 83-84.

21. James Horace Bass, "The Attack upon the Confederate Administration in Georgia in the Spring of 1864," *Georgia Historical Quarterly,* XVIII (1934), 228-229.

22. *Acts of the Georgia General Assembly* (1863; Extra Session, 1864), p. 155.

23. *Acts of the General Assembly of . . . Georgia, . . . November, 1864; Also Extra Session of 1865, . . .* (Milledgeville, 1865), pp. 84-85.

24. *Laws of the Mississippi Legislature* (Called Session, 1862; Regular Session, 1863), pp. 87-89.

25. *Laws of the State of Mississippi, . . .*

Called Session . . . February and March, 1863 (Meridian, 1865), pp. 22-23; *Acts of the Alabama General Assembly* (Called and Regular Sessions, 1863), pp. 13-15; *General Laws of the Texas Legislature* (1863), p. 4; *Acts of the South Carolina General Assembly* (September and December Sessions, 1863), pp. 117-178.

26. *General Laws of the Texas Legislature* (Extra Session, 1863), pp. 26-27; *Acts of the Georgia General Assembly* (1863; Called Session, 1864), p. 63; *Public Laws of the North Carolina General Assembly* (Called Session, 1863), p. 33.

27. Richard Harrison to Governor John Pettus, December 19, 1862, in Mississippi Governors' Papers, State Department of Archives and History.

28. Ella Lonn, *Desertion during the Civil War* (New York, 1928), p. 113.

29. *O. R.*, series IV, III, 706-707.

30. Coulter, *op. cit.*, p. 392.

31. *Acts and Resolutions Adopted by the General Assembly of Florida . . . 1863* (Tallahassee, 1863), pp. 55-56; *Ibid.;* 1864 (First Session), pp. 38-39.

32. Raleigh *Standard*, February 18, 1863; Augusta *Chronicle* and *Sentinel*, March 13, 1864; Atlanta *Daily Intelligencer*, March 24, 1864.

33. *Public Laws of the North Carolina General Assembly* (Adjourned Session, 1862-63), p. 76, 12.

34. *Ibid.* (Called Session, 1863), p. 5.

35. *Journal . . . of the General Assembly of . . . North Carolina, . . . Adjourned Session, ___1864* (Raleigh, 1864), pp. 16-18.

36. *Ibid.*, pp. 43-45.

37. *Public Laws of the North Carolina General Assembly* (Adjourned Session, 1864), pp. 10-11.

38. *Ibid.*, 1865 (Raleigh, 1865), pp. 39-40.

39. *Acts of the Georgia General Assembly* (1863; Called Session, 1864), pp. 45, 152-154.

40. Bass, "The Attack upon the Confederate Administration in Georgia," pp. 228-229.

41. Turnwold *Countryman*, March 29, 1864.

42. Owsley, p. 493.

43. *O. R.*, series IV, I, 479.

44. *Public Laws of the North Carolina General Assembly* (First Extra Session, 1861), pp. 87-90; *Ibid.* (Second Extra Session, 1861), pp. 94-95; *Acts of the Alabama General Assembly* (Second Called and Regular Sessions, 1861), p. 78; *O. R.*, series I, LIII, 775.

45. *O. R.*, series IV, I, 479.

46. *Ibid.*, 705.

47. *Documents of the First Session of the . . . Legislature of the State of Louisiana* (Baton Rouge, 1862), pp. 3-15.

48. *House Journal of the . . . General Assembly of . . . Tennessee, . . . 1861* (Nashville, 1861), pp. 115-119; *Ibid.*, Manuscript, pp. 186-192, Tennessee State Library.

49. *O. R.*, series IV, I, 424.

50. *Ibid.*, 584.

51. *Ibid.*, 624.

52. Hamilton, *The Correspondence of Jonathan Worth*, I, 275-280.

53. *Acts of the South Carolina General Assembly* (September and December Sessions, 1863), p. 188; *Acts of the Alabama General Assembly* (Called and Regular Sessions, 1862), pp. 47-48; *Laws of the Mississippi Legislature* (Called Session, 1862; Regular Session, 1863), pp. 196-197.

54. *O. R.*, series IV, II, 39.

55. *Public Laws of the North Carolina General Assembly* (Adjourned Session, 1863), pp. 75-77.

56. *Acts of the Virginia General Assembly* (1861-62), p. 153.

57. *O. R.*, series IV, II, 469-471.

58. *Acts of the Florida General Assembly* (First Session, 1862), p. 33; *Public Laws of the North Carolina General Assembly* (Adjourned Session, 1863), p. 15; *Laws of the Mississippi Legislature* (Called Session, 1862;

Regular Session, 1863), pp. 156-157; *General Laws of the Texas Legislature* (Called Session, 1864), pp. 12-13; *Acts . . . Called Session, 1864, and . . . Regular Session of the General Assembly of Alabama, . . . 1864* (Montgomery, 1864), pp. 12-13; *Acts . . . of the State of Louisiana, First Session . . . 1864* (Shreveport, 1864), p. 18; *Acts of the Georgia General Assembly* (1863; Extra Session, 1864), pp. 62-63.

59. Cauthen, p. 185.

60. *O. R.*, series IV, II, 988-989.

61. Florida *Sentinel,* December 8, 1863.

62. Bellville *Countryman,* August 2, 1864.

63. Governor John Milton to James Seddon, January 26, 1864, in Milton Letter Books.

64. *O. R.*, series IV, III, 1170.

65. Governor Joseph Emerson Brown to Honorable R. H. Lyon, August 14, 1862, in Governor Joseph Emerson Brown's Letter Book, State Department of Archives. Hereafter cited as Governor Brown's Letter Book.

66. *O. R.*, series IV, II, 470.

67. Cauthen, 148.

68. *Acts of the General Assembly of . . . South Carolina, December, 1862, and February and April, 1863* (Columbia, 1863), pp. 105-108.

69. Cauthen, pp. 178-179.

70. *Ibid.*, pp. 179, 182, 184.

71. Henry H. Creswell to A. G. McGrath, April 8, 1862, in Executive Papers, South Carolina Department of Archives and History.

72. *Acts of the General Assembly of . . . Virginia, Called Session, 1862, . . .* (Richmond, 1862), p. 608.

73. E. R. Turnbull to Colonel George W. Munford, September 19, 1863; B. J. Worsham to Governor John Letcher, September 16, 1863; in Executive Papers, Virginia State Library.

74. Clipping from *Spectator,* dated Richmond, February 1, 1864, signed by J. M. McCue, in Executive Papers, Virginia State Library.

75. *Acts of the Virginia General Assembly* (1863-64), p. 87.

76. *Acts of the Florida General Assembly* (First Session, 1864), pp. 27-28; *Acts of the Alabama General Assembly* (Called and Regular Sessions, 1862), p. 42.

77. Coulter, *op. cit.*, p. 151.

78. *Acts of the Alabama General Assembly* (Called Session, 1861), p. 16.

79. Coulter, *op. cit.*, p. 175.

80. *Acts of the Alabama General Assembly* (Second Called and Regular Sessions, 1861), pp. 20-21.

81. *Ordinances of the Virginia Convention* (April-July Session, 1861), pp. 42, 46.

82. *Acts of the Alabama General Assembly* (Called and Regular Sessions, 1862), pp. 202-203; *Acts of the Florida General Assembly* (First Session, 1862), pp. 78-79; *Laws of the Mississippi Legislature* (Called Session, 1862; 1863), pp. 75-76; *Acts of the South Carolina General Assembly* (December-April Session, 1862-63), pp. 141-42.

83. *General Laws of the Texas Legislature* (Extra Session, 1863), p. 35.

84. Savannah *Daily Morning News,* July 2, 1863.

85. John Christopher Schwab, *The Confederate States of America 1861-65, . . .* (New Haven, 1913), p. 51.

86. *General Laws of the Texas Legislature* (Called Session, 1864), pp. 16-17, 12.

87. Bettersworth, p. 75; *O. R.*, series IV, III, 1162-64.

88. *O. R.*, series IV, III, 685.

89. *Ibid.*, 735.

90. *Acts of the Florida General Assembly* (First Session, 1864), pp. 10-13.

91. *Acts of the Georgia General Assembly* (1864; Extra Session, 1865), pp. 19-20.

Chapter IV

1. Schwab, pp. 126-128.

2. *Public Acts of the Tennessee Gen-*

eral Assembly (First Session, 1861-62), p. 54; *Acts of the Florida General Assembly* (1861), pp. 26-28; *Acts of the Alabama General Assembly* (First Called Session, 1861), pp. 9-11; *Laws of the Mississippi Legislature* (1861-62), p. 162; *Acts of the General Assembly of . . . Virginia, 1861, . . .* [Extra Session] (Richmond, 1861), pp. 123-125.

3. *Public Acts of the Tennessee General Assembly* (Second Extra Session, 1861), pp. 50-53; *Ibid.* (First Session, 1861-62), p. 42.

4. Schwab, pp. 135-137.

5. *Laws of the Mississippi Legislature* (1861-62), pp. 147-163.

6. *Acts of the General Assembly of Georgia, . . . November and December, 1861* (Milledgeville, 1861), pp. 20-21.

7. *Acts of the South Carolina General Assembly* (1861-62), pp. 45-48.

8. Schwab, p. 135.

9. *Acts of the Alabama General Assembly* (Second Called and Regular Sessions, 1861), p. 108; Manuscript, *Public Acts of Tennessee . . . Extra Session* of the *General Assembly* (Memphis, February 20-March 20, 1862), pp. 55-56, on microfilm in Emory University Library; *Private Laws . . . of North Carolina . . . 1860-61* (Raleigh, 1861), pp. 14-31.

10. *Acts of the Virginia General Assembly* (Adjourned Session, 1863), p. 58; *Acts of the Florida General Assembly* (1861), pp. 26-28.

11. Schwab, pp. 134-136.

12. *Journal of the House of Representatives, of . . . Mississippi . . . November and December, 1861, and January, 1862* (Jackson, 1862), pp. 237-238.

13. *Laws of the Mississippi Legislature* (1861-62), pp. 76-77, 227-228.

14. R. C. Parker to Governor John Gills Shorter, February 25, 1862, in Governors' Papers, Alabama State Library.

15. Montgomery *Mail*, February 25, 1863.

16. *Acts . . . of the General Assembly of . . . Arkansas, . . .* [March, 1862] (Little Rock, 1862), pp. 7-8.

17. Tallahassee *Sentinel*, December 8, 1863.

18. Governor Joseph E. Brown to Honorable Linton Stephens, February 25, 1862, in Brown Letter Books, Georgia State Department of Archives.

19. W. K. Mitchell to Governor Joseph Emerson Brown, March 6, 1862, in Telamon Cuyler Collection, University of Georgia Library.

20. *Acts of the General Assembly of . . . Georgia, . . . November and December, 1862; Also Extra Session of 1863* (Milledgeville, 1863), pp. 5-6, 116.

21. Athens *Southern Banner*, April 17, 1863.

22. Gordon Wright, "Economic Conditions in the Confederacy as Seen by the French Consuls," *Journal of Southern History*, VI (1951), 204.

23. *Documents of the Louisiana Legislature* (First Session, 1863), pp. 3-4.

24. New Orleans *Daily Crescent*, January 11, 1862; Natchitoches *Union*, February 6, 1862.

25. A. Mouton to Governor Thomas O. Moore, January 25, 1862, in Thomas O. Moore Papers, Louisiana State University.

26. *Laws of the Mississippi Legislature* (1861-62), pp. 59-66.

27. W. M. Robinson, Jr., "Prohibition in the Confederacy," *American Historical Review,* XXVII (1931), 50.

28. Letter to W. A. Graham, December 8, 1861, in Papers of William Alexander Graham, Southern Historical Collection, University of North Carolina. Hereafter cited as William Alexander Graham Papers.

29. *Ordinances and Resolutions of North Carolina . . . January and*

February, 1862. (Raleigh, 1862), pp. 119-120.

30. *Public Laws of the North Carolina General Assembly* (Adjourned Session, 1862-63), pp. 20-21.

31. *Ibid.*, 1864, pp. 8-9.

32. *Acts of the Arkansas General Assembly* (Special Session, 1862), p. 3; *Ibid.*, 1862, p. 30.

33. General P. G. T. Beauregard to Governor John Milton, October 27, 1863, in Milton Letter Book.

34. *Journal of the Florida Senate* (Second Session, 1863), p. 79.

35. *Acts of the Florida General Assembly* (Second Session, 1863), pp. 44-45.

36. *Journal of the Called Session, 1862, and the Second Regular Session of the House of Representatives of . . . Alabama, . . . , 1862* (Montgomery, 1863), pp. 15-16.

37. *Acts of the Alabama General Assembly* (Called and Regular Sessions, 1863), pp. 98-99.

38. Willie D. Halsell, ed., "Letters of Jacob Faser, Confederate Armorer," *Alabama Historical Quarterly* III (1941), 201.

39. *Acts of the Alabama General Assembly* (Called and Regular Sessions, 1864), pp. 95-101.

40. *Journal of the Georgia Senate* (1862), pp. 17-18.

41. *Laws of the Mississippi Legislature* (Called Session, 1862; 1863), pp. 95-96.

42. *Ibid.*, March and April, 1864 (Meridian, 1864), pp. 63-68.

43. Harris County *Enterprise,* March 30, 1865.

44. *Acts of the Louisiana Legislature* (Extra Session, 1863), pp. 29-30.

45. *Acts of the Virginia General Assembly* (Called Session, 1862), p. 19.

46. Richmond *Whig,* February 25, 1862.

47. *General Laws of the Texas Legislature* (1863), pp. 48-49.

48. Austin *State Gazette,* December 23, 1863.

49. Ella Lonn, *Salt as a Factor in the Confederacy* (New York, 1933), p. 60.

50. Luther Edward Chandler, "The Career of Henry Watkins Allen," pp. 174-76, unpublished Dissertation, Louisiana State University, 1950; Vincent H. Cassidy and Amos E. Simpson, *Henry Watkins Allen of Louisiana* (Baton Rouge, 1964), p. 107.

51. *Acts of the Louisiana Legislature* (First Session, 1861), p. 27.

52. *Ordinances and Resolutions . . . of North Carolina, Second Session in November and December, 1861,* (Raleigh, 1862), pp. 151-152.

53. Hillsborough *Recorder,* September 3, 1862.

54. *Public Laws of the North Carolina General Assembly* (1862-63), pp. 28-30.

55. Hamilton, *The Correspondence of Jonathan Worth,* I, p. 236.

56. *Public Laws of the North Carolina General Assembly 1864-1865* (Raleigh, 1865), pp. 62-63, 72.

57. *Acts of the Alabama General Assembly* (Second Called and Regular Sessions, 1861), p. 29.

58. Thomas J. McClellan to "Bob," November 10, 1861, in Buchanan-McClellan Papers.

59. Mobile *Advertiser and Register,* November 27, 1862.

60. Montgomery *Weekly Mail,* November 22, 1862.

61. Montgomery *Weekly Advertiser,* June 13, 1863.

62. *Acts of the Georgia General Assembly* (1861), pp. 7, 103.

63. Governor Brown to Colonel John Harris, November 27, 1862, in Governor Brown's Letter Book.

64. *Acts of the Georgia General Assembly* (1862; Extra Session, 1863), p. 123.

65. Typescript Diary of Samuel A. Agnew, vol. II, October 27, 1862, in Southern Historical Collection, University of North Carolina.

66. Lonn, *Salt as a Factor in the Confederacy,* pp. 95-96.

67. *General Laws of the Texas Legislature* (1862), pp. 61-62.

68. *Acts of the Virginia General Assembly* (1861-62), pp. 156-157.

69. *Ibid.* (Called Session, 1862), pp. 3-5.

70. Lonn, p. 141.

71. *Acts of the Virginia General Assembly* (Adjourned Session, 1863), pp. 55-56.

72. Washington *Telegraph,* January 29, 1862.

73. *Acts of the Arkansas General Assembly* (1862), pp. 46-47.

74. *Acts of the Alabama General Assembly* (Second Called and Regular Sessions, 1861), pp. 70-71.

75. *Laws of the Mississippi Legislature* (Called Session, 1862; 1863), pp. 143-144.

76. *Acts of the Virginia General Assembly* (Extra Session, 1862), p. 24.

77. *Laws of the Mississippi Legislature* (1861-62), p. 114.

78. *General Laws of the Texas Legislature* (1863), pp. 22-23.

79. *Ordinances of the North Carolina Convention* (1862), p. 122.

80. Richmond *Enquirer,* November 14, 1862.

81. *Acts of the Alabama General Assembly* (Called and Regular Sessions, 1862), p. 49; *Ibid.,* p. 111.

82. *Acts of the Virginia General Assembly* (1863-64), pp. 33-35.

83. *Journal of the Florida Senate* (Second Session, 1863), p. 52 in Appendix.

84. Tallahassee *Sentinel,* April 7, 1863.

85. M. Talbot to Governor Pendleton J. Murrah, February 20, 1866, in Governors' Letters, Texas State Library.

86. *Public Laws of the North Carolina General Assembly* (Called Session, 1863), p. 70.

87. Turnwold *Countryman,* August 30, 1864.

88. Manuscript Executive Minute Book, 1860-1865, in Georgia State Department of Archives and History; Invoice, November 17, 1864, in Telamon Cuyler Collection, University of Georgia.

89. *Public Laws of The North Carolina General Assembly* (Called Session, 1863), p. 69.

90. *Ibid.* (Adjourned Session, 1863), pp. 74-75.

91. J. S. Amis to Governor Zebulon Vance, December 14, 1863, in Vance Papers, 1862-1865, North Carolina Department of Archives and History.

92. *Acts of the South Carolina General Assembly* (September and December, 1863), pp. 195-196.

93. *Journal of the Senate of . . . Mississippi, December 1862, and November 1863* (Jackson, 1864), pp. 95-98.

94. *Acts of the Georgia General Assembly* (1862; Extra Session, 1863), p. 101.

95. Contract, December 10, 1862, in Telamon Cuyler Collection, University of Georgia.

96. John Milton to Governor Joseph E. Brown, March 10, 1863, in Milton Letter Book, Florida Historical Library.

97. Governor F. R. Lubbock to Governor Joseph E. Brown, March 10, 1863, in Governors' Letter Press Book, Texas State Library.

98. *Public Laws of the North Carolina General Assembly* (Adjourned Session, 1862-63), p. 74; Governor Joseph E. Brown to Governor Zebulon Vance, February 4, 1863, in Vance Papers, North Carolina Department of Archives and History.

99. Chandler, vi; see also Cassidy and Simpson, pp. 102-118.

100. Chandler, pp. 169-170.

101. *Acts of the Georgia General Assembly* (1863; Extra Session, 1864), pp. 8-9.

102. *Public Laws of the North Carolina*

General Assembly (Called Session, 1863), p. 72.

103. *Acts of the Virginia General Assembly* (Called Session, 1863), pp. 20-21.

104. Sarah N. Dorsey, *Recollections of Henry Watkins Allen,* . . . (New York, 1866), p. 241; Bragg, pp. 193-195.

105. Robert C. Black, *The Railroads of the Confederacy* (Chapel Hill, 1952), p. 3.

106. *Ibid.,* p. 44; *Public Acts of the Tennessee General Assembly* (Second Extra Session, 1861), p. 36.

107. Charles Lewis Price, "The Railroads of North Carolina during the Civil War," pp. 12-16, unpublished M.A. Thesis, University of North Carolina.

108. *Acts of the South Carolina General Assembly* (1861-62), pp. 57-59, 68-70.

109. Comptroller-General's Report, October 4, 1865, in South Carolina Legislative Papers, 1860-65, South Carolina Department of Archives and History.

110. Montgomery *Mail,* January 25, 1861.

111. *Acts of the Alabama General Assembly* (First Called Session, 1861), pp. 19, 80; *Ibid.* (Second Called and Regular Sessions, 1861), p. 41.

112. Bryan, pp. 110-111; Jas. J. King to Governor Joseph J. Brown, August 19, 1861, in Miscellaneous Confederate Letters, Georgia State Department of Archives and History; "A Soldier" to Governor Joseph E. Brown, December 1, 1862, in Telamon Cuyler Collection, University of Georgia.

113. *Acts of the Arkansas General Assembly* (1862), pp. 86-87.

114. *Acts of the Louisiana Legislature* (First Session, 1861), pp. 46-47.

115. Governor's Message to the House and Senate of Virginia in Executive Papers, Virginia State Library.

116. *Acts of the Virginia General Assembly* (1861-62), pp. 67-71.

117. *Ibid.* (Called Session, 1862), p. 27.

118. *Acts of the Alabama General Assembly* (Second Called and Regular Sessions, 1861), p. 48; *Laws of the Mississippi Legislature* (1861-62), pp. 248-250; *Acts of the Florida General Assembly* (1861), pp. 123-130; *Acts of the Louisiana Legislature* (First Session, 1861), pp. 47-48; *Laws of the Texas Legislature* . . . *Extra Session* (Austin, 1861), p. 25.

119. *Ibid.,* pp. 4, 9, 96; *Ibid.* (1862), pp. 43-44.

120. *Ibid.,* p. 37.

121. *Laws of the Mississippi Legislature* (Called Session, 1864), pp. 9-10.

122. *Acts of the Georgia General Assembly* [called sessions, March and April, 1863] (Milledgeville, 1863), p. 140.

123. *Acts of the Mississippi Legislature* (Called Session, 1862; Regular Session, 1863), pp. 146-147; *General Laws of the Texas Legislature* (1863), pp. 7-8; *Acts of the South Carolina General Assembly* (1864-65), pp. 261-262.

124. *Acts of the Mississippi Legislature* (Called Session, 1862; 1863), pp. 127-128; *Acts of the Georgia General Assembly* (1863; Extra Session, 1864), p. 132.

125. *Acts of the Florida General Assembly* (1860), p. 66.

126. *Acts of the Alabama General Assembly* (Called and Regular Sessions, 1864), p. 77.

127. *Acts of the Florida General Assembly* (1861), pp. 32, 37.

128. *Ibid.* (First Session, 1864), p. 32.

129. *Acts of the Alabama General Assembly* (Second Called and Regular Sessions, 1861), p. 52.

130. *Acts of the Louisiana Legislature* (Extra Session, 1862-63), p. 17; *Public Laws of the North Carolina General Assembly* (1864-65), pp. 38-39.

131. *Acts of the Virginia General As-*

sembly (Adjourned Session, 1863), p. 57.

132. *Ibid.,* 1864, pp. 36-37; Richmond *Examiner,* March 3, 1864.

CHAPTER V

1. *Acts of the Florida General Assembly* (1861), pp. 38-43; *General Laws of the Texas Legislature* (1862), p. 54; *Ordinances of the Arkansas Convention* (May, 1861), pp. 66-68; *Acts of the Arkansas General Assembly* (Special Session, 1862), p. 13; *Ibid.* (Regular Session, 1862), p. 39; *Public Laws of the North Carolina General Assembly* (First Extra Session, 1861), pp. 103-104; *Acts of the Louisiana Legislature* (First Session, 1861), pp. 99-100; *Ibid.* (Second Session, 1861), p. 64.

2. *Ordinances of the Virginia Convention* (April-July Session, 1861), pp. 23-24; *Public Acts of the Tennessee General Assembly* (Second Extra Session, 1861), p. 38; *Public Laws of the North Carolina General Assembly* (1860-61), pp. 39-40; *Acts of the Louisiana Legislature* (Extra Session, 1863), pp. 31-32; *Laws of the Mississippi Legislature* (July, 1861), pp. 67-68; *Laws of the Texas Legislature* (Extra Session, 1863), pp. 20-22.

3. *General Laws of the Texas Legislature* (1861), p. 40; *Acts of the Arkansas General Assembly* (Special Session, 1861), p. 60; *Laws of the Mississippi Legislature* (1861-62), p. 82; *Acts of the Louisiana Legislature* (Second Session, 1861), p. 168.

4. *Acts of the Georgia General Assembly* (1864; Extra Session, 1865), p. 92.

5. Manuscript Report, Committee on Colored Population, House of Representatives, November 29, 1860, in Legislative Papers, South Carolina Department of Archives and History.

6. *Acts of the Georgia General Assembly* (1861), p. 68. This measure amended the Georgia penal code to render a white woman indictable on grounds of adultery or fornication,

as the case might be, who "shall live or cohabit" with a slave or a free Negro.

7. *Ibid.* (1863; Extra Session, 1864), p. 46; General Laws of the Texas Legislature (Called Session, 1864), pp. 4-5; *Laws of the Mississippi Legislature* (Called Session, 1862; Regular Session, 1863), pp. 147-148; *Acts of the Virginia General Assembly (Regular Session, 1863-64),* pp. 39-40; *Public Laws of the North Carolina General Assembly* (1860-61), p. 69.

8. *Acts of the Alabama General Assembly* (Called and Regular Sessions, 1863), pp. 61-62.

9. *Journal of the House of Representatives . . . of Georgia, . . . , March 25th, 1863* (Milledgeville, 1863), pp. 11-12; Edmund Cody Burnett, ed., "Some Confederate Letters: Alabama, Georgia, and Tennessee," *Georgia Historical Quarterly* XXI (1937), 195-197; *Acts of the Georgia General Assembly* (1862; Extra Session, 1863), p. 137.

10. *Ordinances of the Texas Convention* (1861), p. 35.

11. Typescript Journal of Reverend James A. Lyon, Columbus, Mississippi, pp. 112-113, in Mississippi State Department of Archives and History.

12. *Proceedings of the Convention of Florida . . .* [February and April, 1861] (Tallahassee, 1861), pp. 59-60; *Acts of the Florida General Assembly* (First Session, 1864), pp. 7-9.

13. Typescript Diary of John W. Brown, May 5, 1861, microfilm in Southern Historical Collection, University of North Carolina.

14. *Laws of the Mississippi Legislature* (Called Session, July 1861), pp. 70-71.

15. *Acts of the South Carolina General Assembly* (1860-61), pp. 862-863; *Acts of the Alabama General Assembly* (Called and Regular Sessions, 1864), p. 19; *Acts of the Called Session of the General Assembly of . . . Arkan-*

sas . . . , *1864* (Washington, D. C., 1896), pp. 13-14.

16. Brigadier General H. Heth to Governor John Letcher, April 2, 1862, in Executive Papers, Virginia, Virginia State Library.

17. W. H. George to Governor Zebulon Vance, November 21, 1862, in Vance Papers, North Carolina Department of Archives and History.

18. "Soldier's Sister" to Governor Thomas O. Moore, August 9, 1862, in Thomas O. Moore Papers, Louisiana State University.

19. *Acts of the Georgia General Assembly* (1861), p. 43; *Acts of the Alabama General Assembly* (Second Called and Regular Sessions, 1861), p. 197; *Ibid.*, 1862, pp. 54, 229; *Laws of the Mississippi Legislature* (1861), pp. 258-259; *Acts of the Virginia General Assembly* (Called Session, 1863), pp. 17-18; *Acts of the Florida General Assembly* (First Session, 1862), pp. 11, 31-32; *Public Laws of the North Carolina General Assembly* (Adjourned Session, 1864), pp. 6-7; *Ibid.* (Regular Session, 1864-65), pp. 14-15.

20. *Laws of the Mississippi Legislature* (Called Session, 1862; Regular Session, 1863), pp. 148-149; *Ibid* (Regular Session, 1861-1862), p. 203; *Ibid.*, (Called Session, 1864), pp. 42-50; *Acts of the Arkansas General Assembly* (1862), p. 13; *Ibid.* (Called Session, 1864), p. 1; *Acts of the Alabama General Assembly* (Called and Regular Sessions, 1862), pp. 74-75; *General Laws of the Texas Legislature* (Extra Session, 1863), pp. 3-5; *Public Laws of the North Carolina General Assembly* (Adjourned Session, 1862-63), pp. 8-13; *Acts of the Florida General Assembly* (First Session, 1862), pp. 47-50.

21. *Laws of the Mississippi Legislature* (Called Session, 1862; 1863); p. 128.

22. *Ibid.* (Regular Session, 1861), pp. 243-244; *Acts of the Alabama General Assembly* (Called and Regular

Sessions, 1862), pp. 76-77; *Acts of the Florida General Assembly* (First Session, 1864), pp. 16-17; *Acts of the Georgia General Assembly* (1862; Extra Session, 1863), p. 23.

23. *Acts of the Arkansas General Assembly* (Extra Session, 1862), pp. 65-66; *Acts of the Georgia General Assembly* (1861), p. 59; *Ibid.* (1864; Extra Session, 1865), p. 57; *Laws of the Mississippi Legislature* (Called Session, 1862; 1863), pp. 219-220.

24. Petition, January 17, 1861, in South Carolina Legal System Papers, South Carolina Department of Archives and History.

25. Diary of John W. Brown, February 4, 1862, University of North Carolina.

26. Montgomery *Weekly Mail*, January 25, 1861.

27. Thomas J. McClellan to J. M. Moore, November 3, 1861, in Buchanan-McClellan Papers, University of North Carolina.

28. Selma *Reporter*, November 25, 1861.

29. Dallas *Herald*, January 30, 1861.

30. Austin *State Gazette*, November 30, 1861.

31. Petitions in the Legislative Papers, Thirty-third General Assembly, First Session, Tennessee State Library, *Senate Journal of Second Extra Session of the . . . General Assembly of . . . Tennessee, . . . , 1861* (Nashville, 1861), pp. 35-36; Daily Journal of John Houston Bills, June 24, 1861, Southern Historical Collection, University of North Carolina.

32. Raleigh *Standard*, June 15, 1861.

33. James Gwyn's Book and Papers, vol. III, September 18, 1861, in Southern Historical Collection, University of North Carolina.

34. Charles Wilson to William Alexander Graham, January 31, 1862, in William Alexander Graham Papers, University of North Carolina.

35. New Orleans *Daily Crescent*, November 25, December 25, 1861; Shreveport *Semi-Weekly News*, Janu-

ary 14, 1862; New Orleans *Daily Crescent,* January 20, 1862.

36. Lancaster (South Carolina) *Ledger,* February 12, 1862.

37. *Ordinances of the Arkansas Convention* (May Session, 1861), pp. 35-37; *Acts of the Arkansas General Assembly* (1862), pp. 71-72; *Acts of the South Carolina General Assembly* (1860-61), pp. 861-862; *Ibid.* (September and December Sessions, 1863), p. 199.

38. *Journal of the Florida Convention* (January Session, 1861), p. 9; *Acts of the Florida General Assembly* (1860-61), p. 80.

39. *Ibid.,* 1861 (Tallahassee, 1861), pp. 219-222.

40. *Ibid.,* pp. 17-18.

41. Montgomery *Weekly Confederation,* February 15, 1861.

42. Montgomery *Weekly Advertiser,* August 28, 1861.

43. *Acts of the Georgia General Assembly* (1860-61), pp. 21-22.

44. E. I. M. Dyer to Governor John J. Pettus, July 2, 1861; P. H. Gully to Governor John J. Pettus, July 15, 1861, in Governors' Papers, Mississippi Department of Archives.

45. *Acts of the Mississippi Legislature* (Called Session, July, 1861), pp. 74-75.

46. Waco *Southwest,* January 16, 1861.

47. Galveston *News,* April 6, 1861.

48. Bellville *Countryman,* December 4, 1861; *General Laws of the Texas Legislature* (1861), pp. 5-6.

49. *Ibid.,* p. 40.

50. Schwab, p. 109.

51. *Documents of the Louisiana Legislature* (First Session, 1861), pp. 3-4.

52. *Acts of the Louisiana Legislature* (First Session, 1861), p. 40.

53. *Public Acts of the Tennessee General Assembly* (Second Extra Session, 1861), p. 89.

54. *Ibid.* (First Session, 1861-62), pp. 14-18.

55. *Ordinances of the Virginia Conven-*

56. William M. Robinson, *Justice in Grey, a History of the Judicial System of the Confederate States of America* (Cambridge, 1941), p. 119.

57. Patton, p. 29.

58. Typescript Diary of E. H. Reynolds, August 6, 1863, in Lawson McGhee Library.

59. Patton, p. 41.

60. Bryan, pp. 168-196.

61. Bettersworth, p. 114.

62. Bragg, p. 181.

63. Thomas, p. 328.

64. *Laws of the Mississippi Legislature* (Called Session, 1864), p. 38.

65. *Acts of the Arkansas General Assembly* (Called Session, 1864), pp. 2-4, 8-9.

66. *Acts of the Georgia General Assembly* (1864; Extra Session, 1865), p. 51; *Public Laws of the North Carolina General Assembly* (Extra Session, 1863), p. 4; *Ibid.* (Adjourned Session, 1865), pp. 9-10; *General Laws of the Texas Legislature* (Extra Session, 1863), p. 29; *Acts of the Virginia General Assembly* (Adjourned Session, 1863), pp. 71-77.

67. Bryan, p. 222.

68. *Acts of the Georgia General Assembly* (1864; Extra Session, 1865), p. 93.

69. Austin *State Gazette,* September 14, 1861, takes issue with the Dallas *Herald.*

70. Jefferson (Texas) *Confederate News,* May 28, 1864.

71. *Acts of the Louisiana Legislature* (Second Session, 1861), p. 237.

72. *Documents of the Louisiana Legislature* (First Session, 1861), pp. 3-5.

73. *Acts of the Louisiana Legislature* (Second Session, 1865), p. 20.

74. *Ibid.,* 1863 (Extra Session, 1863), p. 37.

75. *Ibid.,* 1865 (Second Session, 1865), p. 26.

76. Bettersworth, pp. 320-322.

77. *Public Laws of the North Carolina*

General Assembly (Second Extra Session, 1861), p. 57.

78. *Journal of the North Carolina Convention* (May Session, 1861), p. 145.

79. Hillsborough (North Carolina) *Recorder*, October 29, 1862.

80 Clement Eaton, *A History of the Southern Confederacy* (New York, 1954), pp. 215-216; *Public Laws of the North Carolina General Assembly* (1864-65), pp. 5-9.

CHAPTER VI

1. *Laws of the Mississippi Legislature* (1861-62), pp. 221-222; *Ibid.* (Called Session, 1865), p. 61; *Acts of the Louisiana Legislature* (First Session, 1861), p. 6; *Public Laws of the North Carolina General Assembly* (Adjourned Session, 1863), p. 30; *Acts of the Florida General Assembly* (Second Session, 1863), p. 58; *Acts of the Georgia General Assembly* (1862; Extra Session, 1863), p. 107.

2. *Acts of the Georgia General Assembly* (1861), p. 61; *Acts of the Alabama General Assembly* (Called Session, 1861), pp. 5-6; *Laws of the Mississippi Legislature* (1861-62), p. 37; *Ordinances of the Arkansas Convention* (May Session, 1861), pp. 35-37; *Acts of the Florida General Assembly* (First Session, 1864), p. 24; *Public Acts of the Tennessee General Assembly* (Extra Session, 1861), p. 43; *General Laws of the Texas Legislature* (1861-62), pp. 5-6; *Acts of the Virginia General Assembly* (1861-62), p. 77; *Acts of the Louisiana Legislature* (First Session, 1862), p. 12; *Ordinances of the North Carolina Convention* (First Session, 1861), p. 35.

3. *Ibid.*, pp. 40-41; *Journal of the Convention of the People of Florida, at a Called Session . . . , 1862* (Tallahassee, 1862), pp. 33-34; *Acts of the Georgia General Assembly* (1861), p. 31; *Ordinances of the Virginia Convention* (April-July Session, 1861), p. 46; *Acts of the South Carolina General Assembly* (1861), pp. 20-21; *Laws of the Mississippi Legislature* (Called Session, 1864), pp. 35-36.

4. *Acts of the Alabama General Assembly* (Second Called and Regular Sessions, 1864), p. 79.

5. Montgomery *Weekly Advertiser,* June 17, 1863.

6. Austin *State Gazette,* October 26, 1861.

7. *Message of Governor F. R. Lubbock to the Extra Session of the Ninth Legislature of the State of Texas. . . .* (Austin, 1863), p. 20.

8. *Acts of the Louisiana Legislature* (First Session, 1861), p. 49; *Ibid.* (Extra Session, 1862-63), pp. 26-27, 31; *Ibid.* (Extra Session, 1863), pp. 4-5; *Ibid.* (Second Session, 1865), pp. 28-29.

9. *Public Laws of the North Carolina General Assembly* (Second Extra Session, 1861), p. 122; *Ibid.* (Adjourned Session, 1862-63), pp. 31-32.

10. *Ibid.* (Adjourned Session, 1864), p. 22.

11. *Acts of the Arkansas General Assembly* (Special Session, 1862), pp. 48-49.

12. *General Laws of the Texas Legislature* (Extra Session, 1863), pp. 11-12; *Ibid.* (Regular Session, 1861-62), p. 13; *Ibid.* (Regular Session, 1863), p. 21; *Ibid.* (Called Session, 1864), p. 18.

13. *Acts of the Florida General Assembly* (First Session, 1862), pp. 53-54, 69; *Ibid.* (Second Session, 1863), pp. 41-12; *Ibid.* (First Session, 1864), p. 15.

14. *Acts of the Virginia General Assembly* (1863-64), pp. 29-30.

15. *Acts of the Georgia General Assembly* (1861), pp. 36-38; *Ibid.* (1863; Extra Session, 1864), pp. 75-76.

16. Lucille Griffith, "Mrs. Juliet Opie Hopkins and Alabama Military Hospitals," *The Alabama Review*, VI (1953), 99-120.

17. *Acts of the Alabama General As-*

sembly (Called and Regular Sessions, 1863), pp. 92, 113-114; *Ibid.* (Called and Regular Sessions, 1864), pp. 13, 33.

18. *Laws of the Mississippi Legislature* (1861), pp. 56-58.

19. *Ibid.* (Called Session, 1862; 1863), pp. 74-75.

20. D. A. Kinchloe, Chief Surgeon to Governor Charles Clark, August 1, 1864, in Governors' Papers, Mississippi Department of Archives.

21. *Acts of the Alabama General Assembly* (Called and Regular Sessions, 1862), pp. 204-205; *Laws of the Louisiana Legislature* (First Session, 1864), p. 73; *Public Laws of the North Carolina General Assembly* 1862-63), p. 54; *Ibid.* (Adjourned Session, 1864), p. 26; *General Laws of the Texas Legislature* (1863), p. 51; *Ibid.* (Extra Session, 1863), pp. 34-35; *Acts of the Florida General Assembly* (First Session, 1862), pp. 63-65; *Ibid.* (Second Session, 1863), p. 51; *Ibid.* (First Session, 1864), pp. 39-40; *Acts of the Virginia General Assembly* (1863-64), pp. 70-83; *Laws of the Mississippi Legislature* (1861-62), pp. 68-69.

22. *Acts of the Georgia General Assembly* (Extra Session, 1863), p. 115.

23. *Acts of the Alabama General Assembly* (Called and Regular Sessions, 1863), p. 109; *Acts of the Louisiana Legislature* (Second Session, 1865), p. 16; *Laws of the Mississippi Legislature* (Called Session, 1864), pp. 14-16.

24. *Acts of the Alabama General Assembly* (Called and Regular Sessions, 1862), pp. 67-78; *Public Laws of the North Carolina General Assembly* (1862-63), p. 44.

25. *Acts of the Georgia General Assembly* (1862; Extra Session, 1863), pp. 104-105.

26. *Acts of the Louisiana Legislature* (Second Session, 1865), p. 42.

27. *Acts of the Virginia General Assembly* (Adjourned Session, 1863), pp. 121-122; *Acts of the Alabama General Assembly* (Called and Regular Sessions, 1864), p. 191; *Laws of the Mississippi Legislature* (1861-62), p. 220; *Acts of the Georgia General Assembly* (1862; Extra Session, 1863), p. 104; *Acts of the Louisiana Legislature* (Extra Session, 1862-63), pp. pp. 49-50.

28. Sarah S. Wright, to Governor Joseph E. Brown, May 27, 1861, in Miscellaneous Confederate Papers, Georgia Department of Archives and History.

29. Montgomery *Weekly Mail*, January 25, 1861.

30. Governor Joseph E. Brown to Colonel Jared I. Whitaker, December 12, 1861, in Governor Brown's Letter Books, Georgia Department of Archives and History.

31. Savannah *Daily Morning News*, March 20, 1863.

32. Milledgeville *Confederate Union*, March 31, 1863.

33. Turnwold *Countryman*, November 29, 1864.

34. *Acts of the Alabama General Assembly* (Called and Regular Sessions, 1861), pp. 42-43.

35. Governor John Gills Shorter to Col. William P. Webb, August 5, 1862, in Governors' Papers, Alabama State Library.

36. Montgomery *Weekly Mail*, November 8, 1862; *Acts of the Alabama General Assembly* (Second Called and Regular Sessions, 1862), pp. 18-20; 44-46; Major L. T. Wright to Governor John Gills Shorter, August 31, 1863, in Governors' Papers, Alabama State Library.

37. *Ordinances of the North Carolina Convention* (Second Session, 1861), pp. 68-70.

38. *Journal of the Convention . . . of North Carolina, Second Session, Held in November and December, 1861* (Raleigh, 1862), p. 8.

39. J. G. De Roulhac Hamilton, ed., *The Papers of Thomas Ruffin* (Raleigh, 1920), III, 260-261.

40. Raleigh *Register*, October 26, 1862.

41. *Public Laws of the North Carolina General Assembly* (1862-63), pp. 53-54.

42. *Acts of the Florida General Assembly* (1861), pp. 8-9.

43. *Journal of the Florida Convention* (Called Session, 1862), p. 35.

44. *Acts of the Florida General Assembly* (Twelfth, First Session, 1862), pp. 36-37.

45. Davis, p. 184.

46. *Acts of the Florida General Assembly* (Twelfth, Second Session, 1863), p. 59.

47. Richmond *Enquirer,* April 18, 1862.

48. Richmond *Dispatch,* September 8, 1863.

49. Younger, p. 107.

50. Richmond *Enquirer,* October 5, 1863.

51. Nashville *Patriot,* October 16, 1861.

52. Diary of John W. Brown, February 18, 1863, in University of North Carolina.

53. B. L. Peel to Governor F. L. Lubbock, December 11, 1861, in Governors' Papers, Texas State Library.

54. *Laws of the Mississippi Legislature* (1861), pp. 144-148.

55. *General Laws of the Texas Legislature* (Regular Session, 1861), p. 56; *Ibid.* (Extra Session, 1863), pp. 22, 27.

56. *Governor's Message, Texas* (Extra Session, 1863), p. 14.

57. *General Laws of the Texas Legislature* (Extra Session, 1863), pp. 10-11.

58. Houston *Tri-Weekly Telegraph,* May 25, 1863.

59. Memorial of the Citizens of the Town and District of Spartanburg to His Excellency F. W. Pickens, Governor of the State of South Carolina, in Francis W. Pickens Papers, Duke University. Hereafter cited as Pickens Papers.

60. Petition, January 1, 1863, in Pickens Papers, Duke University.

61. John Backham to Dr. John C. Tabor, May 30, 1862, in E. P. Smith Papers, South Caroliniana Library.

62. Sumter *Tri-Weekly Watchman,* February 2, 1863.

63. *Acts of the South Carolina General Assembly* (1862-63), pp. 143-144.

64. *Loc. cit.;* Coulter, *op. cit.,* p. 234.

65. *Acts of the South Carolina General Assembly* (1861-62), pp. 15-16; *Acts of the Georgia General Assembly* (1861), p. 131; *Public Laws of the North Carolina General Assembly* (First Extra Session, 1861), pp. 104-105; *Ordinances of the Arkansas State Convention* (May Session, 1861), pp. 66-68; *Acts of the Florida General Assembly* (1861), pp. 12-13; *Acts of the Alabama General Assembly* (Second Called and Regular Sessions, 1861), pp. 3-4, 78-80, 170-171, 226; *Ibid.* (Called and Regular Sessions, 1862), pp. 25-26; *Laws of the Mississippi Legislature* (1861), pp. 53-56; *Acts of the Virginia General Assembly* (1861-62), p. 59.

66. Bragg, p. 196; Bettersworth, pp. 237-239.

67. *Acts of the Georgia General Assembly* (1862), pp. 49-52, 55.

68. *Acts of the Arkansas General Assembly* (1862), pp. 16-17, 75-76; *Acts of the Louisiana Legislature* (Extra Session, 1862-63), pp. 35-36.

69. *Public Laws of the North Carolina General Assembly* (Adjourned Session, 1862-63), pp. 23-24; 63-64.

70. *Acts of the Florida General Assembly* (First Session, 1862), pp. 19-20; *Public Acts of the Tennessee General Assembly* (First Session, 1861-62), pp. 57-58; *Acts of the Alabama General Assembly* (Called and Regular Sessions, 1862), pp. 26-29; *Acts of the South Carolina General Assembly* (1862-63), pp. 137-139.

71. *Journal of the Mississippi Senate* (December Session, 1862; November Session, 1863), p. 95; *Journal of the Called Session, 1863, and the Third Regular Annual Session, of the House of Representatives, of the State of Alabama, . . . , 1863* (Montgomery, 1864), p. 74.

72. *Acts of the South Carolina General Assembly* (September and December Sessions, 1863), pp. 191-194.

73. *Laws of the Mississippi Legislature* (Called Session, 1862; 1863), pp. 60-72, 118-122.

74. *Acts of the Virginia General Assembly* (Called Session, 1863), pp. 21-23.

75. H. H. Cofer to Governor Joseph E. Brown, January 5, 1861, in Telamon Cuyler Collection, University of Georgia.

76. *Arts of the Georgia General Assembly* (1862; Extra Session, 1863), p. 160.

77. *Ibid.* (1864; Extra Session, 1865), pp. 8-11.

78. *Acts of the Louisiana Legislature* (First Session, 1864), pp. 70-71.

79. *Ibid.* (Second Session, 1865), pp. 2, 5-6, 8, 47.

80. C. R. Cox to Governor Pendleton Murrah, February 13, 1864, in Governors' Papers, Texas State Library.

81. W. S. Carpenter to Governor Pendleton Murrah, May 14, 1864; James Barnes to Governor Murrah, September 27, 1864, in Governors' Papers, Texas State Library.

82. *Acts of the Florida General Assembly* (First Session, 1864), p. 37.

83. *Acts of the Virginia General Assembly* (1863-64), pp. 24-25, 44-45.

84. *Acts of the Alabama General Assembly* (Called and Regular Sessions, 1864), pp. 5-7, 58-61, 159-160, 167.

85. *Laws of the Mississippi Legislature* (Called Session, 1864), pp. 53-54.

86. *Ibid.* (Called Session, 1865), pp. 8-10.

87. *Acts of the Alabama General Assembly* (Called and Regular Session, 1863), 84-85.

88. *Acts of the Louisiana Legislature* (First Session, 1864) , pp. 15, 68.

89. *Acts of the Alabama General Assembly* (Called and Regular Sessions, 1863), pp. 83-84; *Ibid.* (Called and Regular Sessions, 1864), p. 12.

90. *Laws of the Mississippi Legislature* (Called Session, 1862; 1863), pp. 79-80.

91. *Acts of the Arkansas General Assembly* (Called Session, 1864), pp. 20-21.

92. *Acts of the Florida General Assembly* (First Session, 1864), pp. 26-27.

93. Citizens of Anderson, Texas, to Governor F. L. Lubbock, March 17, 1862, in Governors' Papers, Texas State Library.

94. *General Laws of the Texas Legislature* (Extra Session, 1863), p. 20.

95. *Acts of the Arkansas General Assembly* (Called Session, 1864), pp. 18-19.

96. *Acts of the Louisiana Legislature* (Extra Session, 1863), pp. 25-26; *Ibid.* (First Session, 1864), pp. 22-24; *Ibid.* (Extra Session, 1865), pp. 40-55; *Laws of the Mississippi Legislature* (Called Session, 1862; 1863), *Acts of the Georgia General Assembly* (1863; Extra Session, 1864), p. 108; *Acts of the Alabama General Assembly* (Second Called and Regular Sessions, 1861), pp. 17-18.

97. Ella Lonn, *Desertion during the Civil War, passim;* Georgia Lee Tatum, *Disloyalty in the Confederacy* (Chapel Hill, 1932), *passim.*

CHAPTER VII

1. Cauthen, p. 188.

2. Charles W. Ramsdell, *Behind the Lines in the Southern Confederacy* (Baton Rouge, 1944), p. 4.

3. *Ibid.,* 116.

4. *Acts of the Alabama General Assembly* (Called Session, January, 1861), pp. 41-43, 81; *Ibid.* (Second Called and Regular Sessions, 1861), p. 12.

5. *Ibid.* (Called and Regular Sessions, 1862), pp. 3, 30-32.

6. Ralph B. Draughon, "Some Aspects of the History of Alabama Bond Issues," *The Alabama Review,* VI (1953), pp. 163-174.

7. *Ordinances of the Arkansas Convention* (May Session, 1861), pp. 55-60.

8. *Public Acts of the Tennessee General Assembly* (Second Extra Session, 1861), p. 23.

9. *Acts of the Florida General Assembly* (1860), p. 36; Davis, pp. 179-181.
10. *Acts of the Florida General Assembly* (1861), pp. 71-72.
11. Davis, p. 181.
12. *Acts of the Georgia General Assembly* (1860), p. 49.
13. Governor Joseph E. Brown to R. R. Cuyler, April 24, 1861, in Governors' Letter Books, Georgia Department of Archives and History.
14. *Acts of the Georgia General Assembly* (1861), pp. 3, 65.
15. Governor Joseph E. Brown to R. R. Cuyler, December 30, 1861, in Governors' Letter Books, Georgia Department of Archives and History.
16. *Arts of the Louisiana Legislature* (First Session, 1861), pp. 29, 84-86.
17. Bragg, p. 96.
18. *Acts of the Louisiana Legislature* (First Session, 1864), pp. 11-12.
19. Shreveport *Semi-Weekly News,* February 10, 1864.
20. Bragg, p. 193.
21. *Journal of the Mississippi Convention* (January Session, 1861), pp. 56-57.
22. *Ibid.,* pp. 122-126.
23. Bettersworth, p. 95.
24. *Laws of the Mississippi Legislature* (Called Session, 1864), pp. 21-24.
25. *Ordinances of the North Carolina Convention* (First Session, 1861), pp. 42-45; *Public Laws of the North Carolina General Assembly* (First Extra Session, 1861), pp. 91-94.
26. Hillsborough *Recorder,* February 25, 1862.
27. *Public Laws of the North Carolina General Assembly* (Adjourned Session, 1863), p. 21; *Ibid.* (1864), p. 26.
28. Treasurer's Report, Document 2, Session of 1864-65, in *Legislative Documents, 1864-65, 1865-66* (North Carolina). These Documents are bound together with no title page, in Southern Historical Collection, University of North Carolina.
29. Cauthen, p. 190; *Acts of the South Carolina General Assembly* (1860-61), pp. 937-941, 951-953; *Ibid.* (1861), pp. 26-28.
30. Cauthen, p. 191.
31. *Loc. cit.*
32. *Laws of the Texas Legislature* (Extra Session, 1861), p. 24.
33. *Ibid.,* pp. 39-42.
34. Manuscript Appointment, May 13, 1861, in Governors' Papers, Texas State Library.
35. *General Laws of the Texas Legislature* (1862), p. 42.
36. By the terms of the Compromise of 1850, Texas had received $10,000,000 in United States five per cent bonds. The two Texas Military Boards received 634 of these bonds valued at $634,000 for sale in Mexico and Europe. Approximately 200 of the bonds were sold and accounted for. See Edmund Thornton Miller, "The State Finances of Texas during the Civil War," *Southwestern Historical Quarterly,* XIV (1910), 4-5.
37. *General Laws of the Texas Legislature* (1863), p. 9.
38. Schwab, p. 309.
39. *Acts of the Alabama General Assembly* (Called Session, 1861), pp. 16-17.
40. Mobile *Advertiser and Register,* November 14, 1862.
41. *Acts of the Alabama General Assembly* (Called and Regular Sessions, 1864), pp. 54-56.
42. *Acts of the Arkansas General Assembly* (1862), p. 14.
43. *Ibid.,* p. 74; Washington *Telegraph,* February 19, 1862.
44. *Acts of the Florida General Assembly* (1860), p. 43.
45. *Ibid.* (First Session, 1862), pp. 51-52.
46. Davis, p. 181.
47. *Journal of the Georgia Senate* (1862), pp. 6-9.
48. *Acts of the Georgia General Assembly* (1862; Extra Session, 1863),

pp. 20-21; *Ibid.* (1863); Extra Session, 1864), pp. 14-15.

49. Bryan, p. 56.

50. *Acts of the Louisiana Legislature* (First Session, 1861), pp. 84-86.

51. *Ibid.* (Extra Session, 1862-63), pp. 39-40; *Ibid.* (First Session, 1864), p. 22.

52. Bragg, p. 194.

53. *Journal of the Mississippi Convention* (January Session, 1861), p. 127.

54. *Laws of the Mississippi Legislature* (1861-62), pp. 59-66.

55. Bettersworth, p. 105; Richard Cecil Todd, *Confederate Finance* (Athens, 1954), p. 39.

56. *Laws of the Mississippi Legislature* (1862-63), pp. 286-288.

57. *Journal of the Senate of the State of Mississippi, Called Session, March and April, 1864.* (Meridian, 1864), pp. 6-11.

58. *Laws of the Mississippi Legislature* (Called Session, August, 1864), pp. 21-23, 22-24.

59. *Ordinances of the North Carolina Convention* (First Session, 1861), p. 59; *Public Laws of the North Carolina General Assembly* (First Extra Session, 1861), pp. 91-94.

60. Schwab, p. 152.

61. *Public Laws of the North Carolina General Assembly* (Second Extra Session, 1861), pp. 16-18, 46-47; *Ordinances and Resolutions Passed by the State Convention of North Carolina. Fourth Session in April and May, 1862* (Raleigh, 1862).

62. Wilmington *Journal*, November 20, 1862; *Public Laws of the North Carolina General Assembly* (Regular Session, 1862), pp. 35-38.

63. *Ibid.* (Adjourned Session, 1863), pp. 70-71.

64. *Ibid.* (Adjourned Session, 1864), p. 15; Schwab, p. 152.

65. *Acts of the South Carolina General Assembly* (1860-61), pp. 837-841; *Acts of the General Assembly of . . . South Carolina . . . December*

ber, *1862, and February and April, 1863* (Columbia, 1863), p. 150.

66. *Acts of the South Carolina General Assembly* (1861), pp. 21-22.

67. *Public Acts of the Tennessee General Assembly* (Second Extra Session, 1861), pp. 41-42.

68. J. T. Allen to Daley Daugherty, April 30, 1861, in John T. Allen Letters, 1858-1860, Eugene C. Barker Library, University of Texas.

69. Austin *State Gazette*, November 16, 1861.

70. *General Laws of the Texas Legislature* (1862), p. 37.

71. G. H. Wooten to B. H. Epperson, no date, in B. E. Epperson Manuscripts, Eugene C. Barker Library, University of Texas.

72. *General Laws of the Texas Legislature* (First Called Session, 1864), pp. 10-11.

73. *Loc. cit.*

74. Austin *State Gazette*, September 21, 1864; November 26, 1864.

75. H. R. Latimer to Governor Pendleton J. Murrah, November 24, 1862, in Governors' Letters, Texas State Library.

76. *Acts of the Virginia General Assembly* (Extra Session, 1861), pp. 29-30; *Ibid.* (1861-62), p. 2; Schwab, pp. 152-153.

77. Jeremiah Morton to J. J. Halsey, March 25, 1863, in Morton-Halsey Papers, University of Virginia Library.

78. Richmond *Enquirer*, November 3, 1863; Schwab, pp. 152-153.

79. Davis, p. 185.

80. *Acts of the Alabama General Assembly* (Called and Regular Sessions, 1862), pp. 4-17.

81. *Ibid.* (Called and Regular Sessions, 1863), pp. 74-75.

82. *Ibid.* (Called and Regular Sessions, 1864), p. 51.

83. *Acts of the Arkansas General Assembly* (Special Session, 1861), p. 18.

84. *Ibid.*, pp. 55-56.
85. *Ibid.* (1862), p. 59.
86. Washington *Telegraph*, December 10, 1862.
87. *Acts of the Arkansas General Assembly* (Called Session, 1864), p. 17.
88. *Acts of the Georgia General Assembly* (1861), p. 78.
89. *Ibid.* (1862; Extra Session, 1863), pp. 56-57.
90. *Ibid.*, p. 13.
91. Athens *Southern Banner*, March 27, 1863; *Acts of the Georgia General Assembly* (1862; Extra Session, 1863), pp. 176-178.
92. Savannah *Daily Morning News*, October 1, 1963.
93. *Acts of the Georgia General Assembly* (1863; Extra Session, 1864), pp. 80-81.
94. *Ibid.* (1864); Extra Session, 1865), pp. 65-66.
95. J. Horace Bass, "Civil War Finance in Georgia," *The Georgia Historical Quarterly*, XXVI (1942), 213-224.
96. *Acts of the Georgia General Assembly* (1864; Extra Session, 1865), pp. 18-19.
97. *Acts of the Louisiana Legislature* (First Session, 1861), p. 79.
98. *Ibid.* (Extra Session, 1862-63), O. 20.
99. *Ibid.*, p. 32.
100. *Ibid.* (Second Session, 1865), pp. 43-45, 54-55.
101. *Journal of the Mississippi Convention* (January Session, 1861), pp. 48-53.
102. *Laws of the Mississippi Legislature* (Called Session, July, 1861), pp. 31-34.
103. *Ibid.* (1861-62), p. 261.
104. *Ibid.* (Called Session, 1862; 1863), pp. 77, 111-112, 138.
105. *Ibid.*, pp. 113-122, 153-155.
106. *Ibid.* (Called Session, 1865), pp. 3-10.
107. *Public Laws of the North Carolina General Assembly* (Second Extra Session, 1861), pp. 57-58.
108. *Ordinances of the North Carolina Convention* (Third Session, 1862), p. 127.
109. *Public Laws of the North Carolina General Assembly* (Adjourned Session, 1863).
110. W. W. Hampton to J. George, January 25, 1863, in James Gwyn Books & Papers, 1844-1884, Southern Historical Collection, University of North Carolina.
111. *Public Laws of the North Carolina General Assembly* (1864-65), pp. 26-62.
112. Cauthen, p. 191.
113. Typescript Diary of David Gavin, January 26, 1861, Southern Historical Collection, University of North Carolina.
114. Cauthen, p. 192.
115. *Acts of the South Carolina General Assembly* (September and December Sessions, 1863), pp. 231-234.
116. Cauthen, p. 194.
117. *Public Acts of the Tennessee Legislature* (First Session, 1861-62), p. 36.
118. Dallas *Herald*, February 20, 1861.
119. Galveston *News*, April 6, 1861.
120. *General Laws of the Texas Legislature* (Extra Session, 1861), pp. 51-52.
121. *Ibid.* (1862), pp. 50-51.
122. Houston *Tri-Weekly Telegraph*, January 19, 1863.
123. *General Laws of the Texas Legislature* (Extra Session, 1863), pp. 23-24.
124. Schwab, p. 304.
125. *Acts of the Virginia General Assembly* (Extra Session, 1861), pp. 3-20.
126. *Ibid.* (1861-62), pp. 1-22.
127. Richmond *Enquirer*, January 3, 1863.
128. Schwab, p. 304.
129. Richmond *Enquirer*, January 3, 1863; February 29, 1864.
130. Bettersworth, p. 111; Bryan, p. 57; John T. Allen to D. C. Osborn, no date, in John T. Allen Letters,

the Eugene C. Barker Library, University of Texas.

131. *Journal of the House of Representatives of . . . Georgia . . ., 1861* (Milledgeville, 1862), pp. 210-211.

132. *Journal of the Georgia Senate* (1862), pp. 18-19.

133. *Laws of the Mississippi Legislature* (Called Session, 1862; 1863), p. 178; *Ibid.* (Called Session, 1865), p. 14; *Public Laws of the North Carolina General Assembly* (Adjourned Session, 1865, pp. 16-18; *General Laws of the Texas Legislature* (1862), pp. 40-43; *Acts of the Virginia General Assembly* (Called Session, 1863), pp. 8-10.

134. *Acts of the Louisiana Legislature* (First Session, 1864), pp. 60-63.

135. *Acts of the South Carolina General Assembly* (December Session, 1862; February-April Session, 1863), pp. 92-99.

136. *Public Laws of the North Carolina General Assembly* (Adjourned Session, 1862), p. 24.

137. *Acts of the Louisiana Legislature* (First Session, 1864), pp. 56-57.

138. *Acts of the Georgia General Assembly* (1861), p. 72.

139. *Acts of the South Carolina General Assembly* (September and December Sessions, 1863), pp. 209-219.

CHAPTER VIII

1. Diary of William Augustus Drennan, July 21, 1863, in Mississippi State Department of Archives and History.

2. Lonn, *Desertion during the Civil War*, p. 226.

3. *Ibid.*, pp. 226-229.

4. Nashville *Patriot,* January 31, 1861.

5. Ramsdell, p. 39.

6. General Gideon Pillow to Governor Isham Harris, May 25, 1861, in Harris Papers, Tennessee State Library.

7. *Acts of the Georgia General Assembly* (1861), pp. 69-70; *Public*

Laws of the North Carolina General Assembly (Second Extra Session, 1861), pp. 15-16.

8. Governor John Milton to I. Wood, February 2, 1863, in Milton Letter Book, 1861-1863, Florida Historical Society Library, University of Florida.

9. A. M. Brett to Honorable Joseph E. Brown, March 4, 1862, in Telamon Cuyler Collection, University of Georgia Library.

10. J. Addison Denny to Governor F. L. Lubbock, January 5, 1862, in Governor Lubbock's Letters, Texas State Library.

11. Ramsdell, pp. 59-60.

12. P. L. Rainwater, ed., "Letters of James Lusk Alcorn," *Journal of Southern History,* III (1937), 196-209.

13. Baskerville & Whitfield to Governor Charles Clark, December 18, 1863, in Governors' Papers, Mississippi State Department of Archives and History.

14. *Journal of the House of Representatives of . . . Mississippi, Called Session . . ., February and March, 1865* (Meridian, 1865), pp. 43-45.

15. *Ibid.* (Called Session, 1865), p. 87.

16. Schwab, pp. 126, 259-260.

17. *Ibid.*, pp. 260-261.

18. Albert D. Richardson, *The Secret Service, the Field, the Dungeon, and the Escape* (Hartford, 1866), p. 27.

19. H. S. Fulkerson, *A Civilian's Recollections of the War between the States* (Baton Rouge, 1939), pp. 7-9.

20. E. Merton Coulter, *William G. Brownlow, Fighting Parson of the Southern Highlands* (Chapel Hill, 1937), p. 162.

21. Tatum, pp. 3-4.

22. Bragg, pp. 257-259.

23. Tatum, pp. 44-53.

24. *Ibid,* p. 24.

25. Houston *Tri-Weekly Telegraph,* October 27, 1862; Claude Elliott, "Union Sentiment in Texas 1861-1865," *Southwestern Historical*

Quarterly I (1947), 449-477; C. W. Raines, ed., *Six Decades in Texas or Memoirs of Francis Richard Lubbock, Governor of Texas in Wartime,* . . . Austin, 1900), p. 314.

26. Selma *Morning Reporter,* November 20, 1862.

27. C. C. Clay, Jr., to Governor John Gills Shorter, May 28, 1862, in Governors' Papers, Alabama Department of Archives and History, Montgomery, Alabama.

28. Edward Younger, *op cit.,* p. 73.

29. John Clisby to Governor John Gills Shorter, July 22, 1863, in Governors' Papers, Alabama Department of Archives and History, Montgomery, Alabama.

30. Tatum, pp. 25.

31. *Ibid.,* pp. 107, 135, 155.

32. *Journal of the House of Commons of North Carolina,* . . . *Adjourned Session, 1862-63* (Raleigh, 1863), pp. 26-28.

33. Richard B. Yates, "Governor Vance and the Peace Movement," *North Carolina Historical Review,* XVII (1940), 20.

34. *Public Acts of the North Carolina General Assembly* (Adjourned Session, 1864), pp. 20-21.

35. *Journal of the Senate of the General Assembly of* . . . *North Carolina.* . . . *1864-65* (Raleigh, 1866), pp. 66-67, 87-88.

36. La Grange (Texas) *Patriot,* January 21, 1865.

37. Jacksonville (Florida) *Peninsula,* April 14, 1864.

38. *Loc. cit.*

39. *Journal of the House of Representatives of* . . . *Georgia,* . . ., *1864* (Milledgeville, 1865).

40. Hill, pp. 230-233.

41. Turnwold *Countryman,* February 14, 1865.

42. Memphis *Daily Appeal,* October 12, 1864.

43. Cauthen, p. 218.

44. *Ibid.,* p. 220.

★

BIBLIOGRAPHICAL NOTES

GOVERNMENT DOCUMENTS

SOUTHERN STATE legislatures convened in 75 sessions during the period of secession and the Confederacy. The work of these sessions was recorded in 225 separate documents: laws, senate journals, and house journals. These documents, published or unpublished, comprise the basic materials for this study. Southern state conventions met in 27 sessions. The conventions carried on legislative functions and through their ordinances made adjustments to the new order. Published ordinances and convention journals provided approximately 50 volumes of primary sources for the study.

Fortunately for the historian who would delve into states' legislative programs, records do not have to be traced to the numerous and scattered depositories where the originals repose. A project begun some years ago by the Library of Congress and the University of North Carolina has made state documents available through microphotography. The filmed state records are listed and described in Lillian A. Hamrick, ed., *A Guide to the Microfilm Collection of Early State Records Prepared by the Library of Congress in Association with the University of North Carolina, Collected and Compiled under the Direction of William Sumner Jenkins* (Library of Congress, 1950), and a supplementary guide published in 1951.

The Jenkins' Guide lacks only a few of the legislative records of the Confederate period. It does not list the North Carolina and the Georgia records, nor does it cover all extant documents for Alabama, Tennessee, and Virginia. These were used in the original at the Emory University Library, which obtained through inter-library loan needed volumes. The house and senate journals of the Louisiana 27th Legislature held at Opelousas, Louisiana, in December and January, 1862-63, are in private collections. The last session of the journal of the Virginia House of Delegates is incomplete, breaking off with the adjournment on January 27, 1865. The manuscript house journal of the adjourned session of Tennessee's Thirty-Fourth General Assembly meeting in Memphis, Tennessee, February 20 through March 20, 1862, was lost; as was the manuscript journal of the Texas house for the Ninth Legislature, November 4, 1861, to January 14, 1862. These gaps in the records have been filled to some extent by information gleaned from newspapers and other sources.

Federal documents used included the United States War Department compilations, *The War of the Rebellion: A Compilation of the Official Records of the Union and Confederate Armies* (128 vols., Washington, 1880-1901). Of the 128 volumes, those appearing in Series IV, dealing with state correspondence, were especially valuable. It has been necessary from time to time, to check Confederate statutes in J. M. Matthews, ed., *Statutes at Large of the Confederate Congress* (Richmond 1862-1864) and in Charles W. Ramsdell, ed., *Laws and Joint Resolutions of The Last Session of the Confederate Congress* (November 7, 1864-March 18, 1865) *Together with the Secret Acts of Previous Congresses* (Durham, 1941).

OFFICIAL MANUSCRIPTS

THE SEARCH FOR PERTINENT manuscript material involved work in the libraries, archives, and universities of the Southern states. The Alabama Department of Archives and History contains governors' papers for the entire period. The Department of Archives at Louisiana State University has a good collection of the papers of Thomas Overton Moore, governor of Louisiana, 1860-1864. Florida depositories contain two gubernatorial collections: Governor John Milton's Letter Book, 1861-1863, at the Florida Historical Society Library, University of Florida; and the Governor's Letter Book, Commissary Activities and Correspondence, 1863-1865, in the Florida State Library. The latter library has a manuscript volume containing the opinions of the Florida attorney generals, 1859-1886.

The State Library at Austin, Texas, has a mine of official manuscripts in the incoming letters to the Confederate governors, executive record books kept by the governors, 1861-1865, and letter press books for the period 1863-1865. The microfilm collection at the Eugene C. Barker Library, University of Texas, includes the George A. Trenholm, Francis W. Pickens and M. L. Bonham Papers, 1860-1864, from the Library of Congress; and the Francis W. Pickens Papers, from the Duke University Library.

The Mississippi State Department of Archives and History has preserved papers of the Confederate governors and legislatures. The Tennessee State Library has files of legislative committee reports, petitions, messages and other state manuscripts. The papers of Governor Isham G. Harris in that depository throw valuable light on the government of Tennessee during the Confederate period.

Governors' papers in the North Carolina State Department of Archives and History at Raleigh cover the administrations of John W. Ellis, who died in the summer of 1861, Henry T. Clark, who served until the next election in 1862, and Zebulon B. Vance, 1862-1865. These and the Vance letter books were useful, as were to a lesser degree the legislative papers, 1861-1865.

Virginia State Library holdings include a collection of the executive manuscripts of Governor John Letcher, 1861-1864, and Governor William Smith, 1864-1865. The South Carolina Department of Archives and History has files of official papers, both legislative and executive, for the administrations of Francis W. Pickens, Milledge L. Bonham and A. G. Magrath, 1860-1865.

Official papers of Confederate Georgia are available in the State Department of Archives and History and at the University of Georgia. Governor Joseph B. Brown's executive department minutes and letter books are in the former; and many letters to the governor and miscellaneous state papers are in the Telamon Cuyler Collection, University of Georgia. Information gleaned from manuscripts in the Arkansas Historical Commission was disappointingly meager, but some items of interest appeared in the Kie Oldham Papers.

OTHER MANUSCRIPTS

Manuscript collections in Southern libraries and archives yielded many informative commentaries on state and local affairs. The Southern Historical Collection at the University of North Carolina was useful not only for the state of North Carolina but for its cache of letters and papers written by contemporaries in other areas. The Buchanan-McClellan Papers contain letters written by an Alabama legislator. The typescript diary of David Gavin, a journal written by John Houston Bills, a typescript diary of Reverend Overton Bernard, a typescript diary of Samuel A. Agnew, and a typescript diary of John W. Brown on film in the North Carolina Collection give viewpoints on current affairs of a South Carolinian, a Tennessean, a Virginian, a

Mississippian and an Arkansan, respectively. North Carolina materials used in this depository include the James Gwyn Books and Papers, the Papers of William Alexander Graham, the Papers of James Graham Ramsay, the Alfred E. Willard Papers, the Leander Quincy Sharpe Papers and the George Whitaker Wills Papers. Manuscripts studied at Duke University included the Jesse Turner Letters (Arkansas), the Herschel Vespasian Johnson Papers (Georgia), the Wier Boyd Letters (Georgia) and the Eugenius A. Nisbet Letters and Papers (Georgia).

The Georgia Department of Archives and History possesses a file of Miscellaneous Confederate Papers which proved both interesting and helpful. The Mississippi State Department of Archives and History supplied the typescript Journal of James A. Lyon, Presbyterian minister of Columbus, Mississippi. Items of interest were found also in the D. P. Smith Papers, South Caroliniana Library, University of South Carolina; the typescript Civil War Diary of F. H. Reynolds, Lawson McGhee Library, Knoxville, Tennessee; the B. H. Apperson Manuscripts, the John T. Allen Letters and the Austin-McKinney Papers in the Eugene C. Barker Library, University of Texas; and the Tucker-Harrison-Smith Papers and the Edward Callohill Burks Letters in the University of Virginia library.

Several masters and doctoral theses were consulted in the preparation of this study. Among them were Robert Pattison Folger's "Texas in the War for Southern Independence 1861-1865," University of Texas, doctoral thesis, 1935; Lowry Price Ware, "The South Carolina Executive Councils of 1861 and 1862," University of South Carolina, master's thesis, 1952; Joel R. Williamson, "The Disruption of State Government in South Carolina during the Magrath Administration," University of South Carolina, master's thesis, 1951; Charles Lewis Price, "The Railroads of North Carolina during the Civil War," University of North Carolina, master's thesis, 1951; Luther Edward Chandler, "The Career of Henry Watkins Allen," Louisiana State University, doctoral thesis, 1940; and William Lamar Gammon II, "Governor John Milton of Florida, Confederate States of America," University of Florida, doctoral thesis, 1948.

NEWSPAPERS

Newspapers served as excellent sources for reaction to legislative programs and to state leadership. County weeklies were drawn upon heavily to supplement information found in the more prominent newspapers in an effort to arrive at a cross section of public opinion throughout the states.

Some of the Georgia newspapers used were the Athens *Southern Banner,* the Atlanta *Georgia Literary and Temperance Crusader,* the Augusta *Constitutionalist,* the Milledgeville *Southern Federal Union* (after 1862 the *Confederate Union*), the Milledgeville *Southern Recorder* and the Savannah *Daily Morning News.* Louisiana newspapers offering commentaries on state politics were the Baton Rouge *Daily Advocate,* the New Orleans *Daily Crescent,* the Shreveport *Semi-Weekly News;* Alabama papers of importance for this study were the Montgomery *Weekly Advertiser, Weekly Mail* and *Daily Post,* the Mobile *Advertiser and Register* and the Selma *Daily Reporter.*

At the University of Texas, it was possible to take a good sampling of editorial comment from all sections of the state. The Dallas *Herald,* the Galveston *News and Civilian and Gazette,* the Houston *Tri-Weekly Telegraph* and the Austin *State Gazette* were especially useful.

North Carolina papers studied included the Raleigh *State Journal, Weekly Register* and *Standard* and the Wilmington *Daily Journal;* Virginia papers included the Richmond *Daily Dispatch, Enquirer, Examiner* and *Whig.*

Other newspapers that proved helpful in this study were: The *Des Arc* (Arkansas), *Weekly Citizens* and the Washington (Arkansas) *Telegraph;* the Tallahassee (Florida) *Sentinel* and Jacksonville (Florida) *Peninsula;* the Jackson (Mississippi) *Daily Mississippian;* the Nashville (Tennessee) *Patriot* and Memphis (Tennessee) *Daily Appeal;* and the Charleston (South Carolina) *Mercury* and *Courier.*

PRINTED CORRESPONDENCE
DIARIES, JOURNALS AND MEMOIRS

Professor J. G. De Roulhac Hamilton has edited two valuable collections of letters: *The Correspondence of Jonathan Worth* (2 vols., Raleigh, 1909) and *The Papers of Thomas Ruffin* (4 vols., Raleigh, 1918-20). Another rich North Carolina compilation is in Aubrey Lee Brooks and Hugh Talmage Lefler, eds., *The Papers of Walter Clark* (2 vols., Chapel Hill, 1948). Other printed letters of value are found in Ulrich B. Phillips, ed., *The Correspondence of Robert Toombs, Aexander H. Stephens, and Howell Cobb,* American Historical Association *Annual Report, 1911,* vol. II (Washington, 1913); James D. Waddell, ed., *Biographical Sketch of Linton Stephens, containing a Selec-*

tion of His Letters, Speeches, State Papers, Etc. (Atlanta, 1877); and Mary C. Simms Oliphant and others, eds., *The Letters of William Gilmore Simms* (4 vols., Columbia, 1952-55).

Journals, diaries and memoir material all too often lean heavily in the military news and observations, leaving unrecorded the reactions to the local scene and government. Some exceptions to this rule are found in the following accounts: John Q. Anderson, ed., *Brokenburn, The Journal of Kate Stone 1861-1868* (Baton Rouge, 1955); Sarah A. Dorsey, *Recollections of Henry Watkins Allen, Brigadier-General Confederate Army, Ex-Governor of Louisiana* (New York, 1866); Albert D. Richardson, *The Secret Service. The Field, the Dungeon, and the Escape* (Hartford, 1866); C. W. Raines, ed., *Six Decades in Texas or Memoirs of Francis Richard Lubbock, Governor of Texas in War-time, 1861-63, a Personal Experience in Business, War, and Politics* (Austin, 1900); and Edward Younger, ed., *Inside the Confederate Government. The Diary of Robert Garlick Hill Kean* (New York, 1957).

GENERAL AND SPECIAL STUDIES

Library shelves teem with old and new studies of the Confederacy and of special aspects of Confederate problems. Only a few of the basic monographic and general histories can be mentioned here.

Of primary importance in the study of various legislatures were the following state histories: Charles Edward Cauthen, *South Carolina Goes to War 1860-1865* (Chapel Hill, 1950); T. Conn Bryan, *Confederate Georgia* (Athens, 1953); Jefferson Davis Bragg, *Louisiana in the Confederacy* (Baton Rouge, 1941); and John K. Bettersworth, *Confederate Mississippi, The People and Policies of a Cotton State in Wartime* (Baton Rouge, 1943). Walter L. Fleming, *Civil War and Reconstruction in Alabama* (Cleveland, 1911) falls short of the demands of present day scholarship but is valuable for the tremendous scope of its coverage. William Watson Davis, *The Civil War and Reconstruction in Florida* (New York, 1913) makes wide use of newspaper sources as well as other basic research materials and gives especial attention to the extended range of state responsibilities. David Y. Thomas, *Arkansas in War and Reconstruction 1861-1874* (Little Rock, 1926) is inadequately documented but its treatment of economic problems in the state renders it useful. James Welch Patton, *Unionism and Reconstruction in Tennessee*

1860-1867 (Chapel Hill, 1934) contains some information about the Confederate state government.

Among the numerous studies of special problems of the Confederacy the following were especially helpful: Frank Lawrence Owsley, *State Rights in the Confederacy* (Chicago, 1925); Bell Irvin Wiley, *Southern Negroes 1861-1865* (New Haven, 1938) ; Albert Burton Moore, *Conscription and Conflict in the Confederacy* (New York, 1924) ; Georgia Lee Tatum, *Disloyalty in the Confederacy* (Chapel Hill, 1934); Robert C. Black, III, *The Railroads of the Confederacy* (Chapel Hill, 1952) ; Ella Lonn, *Salt as a Factor in the Confederacy* (New York, 1933) ; Ella Lonn, *Desertion During the Civil War* (New York, 1920); Richard Cecil Todd, *Confederate Finance* (Athens, 1954) ; John Christopher Schwab, *The Confederate States of America 1861-1865* (New Haven, 1913), and Charles W. Ramsdell, *Behind the Lines in the Southern Confederacy* (Baton Rouge, 1944).

The general histories of the Confederacy most useful in this study were E. Merton Coulter, *The Confederate States of America 1861-1865* (Baton Rouge, 1950) and Clement Eaton, *A History of the Southern Confederacy* (New York, 1954).

Biographies of public figures important in state politics from 1860-1865 usually follow the birth-to-death plan and give sketchy coverage of the period of the Confederacy. Exceptions are Louise Biles Hill, *Joseph E. Brown and the Confederacy* (Chapel Hill, 1939), and Richard E. Yates, *The Confederacy and Zeb Vance* (Tuscaloosa, 1948) which are valuable not only for their factual but for their interpretive studies of the problems involved in state and Confederate conflicts.

MAGAZINE ARTICLES

Each of the states that belonged to the Southern Confederacy has its historical magazine; and most of these magazines contain many articles dealing with the states' activities during the Civil War period. *The Journal of Southern History, The Mississippi Valley Historical Review* and *The American Historical Review* also provided a number of useful articles.

Both the *Alabama Review* and the *Alabama Historical Quarterly* have published articles and letters on Confederate Alabama, among which are Willie D. Halsell, ed., "Letters of Jacob Faser, Confederate Armorer," *Alabama Historical Quarterly,* III (1941), 193-202; Lucille Griffith, "Mrs. Juliet Opie Hopkins and Alabama Military Hospitals," *Alabama Review a Quarterly*

Journal of Alabama History, VI (1953), 99-120, *The Georgia Historical Quarterly* supplied many informative articles, one of which was by J. Horace Bass, "Civil War Finance in Georgia," *Georgia Historical Quarterly,* XXVI (1942), 213-24. The Louisiana historical publication offered, among other treatises, Van D. Oden, "The Political Career of Thomas Overton Moore, Secession Governor of Louisiana," *Louisiana Historical Quarterly,* XXVI (1943) 975-1054.

Helpful articles in the *North Carolina Historical Review* included Elizabeth Yates Webb, "Cotton Manufacturing and State Regulation in North Carolina, 1861-65," *North Carolina Historical Review,* IX (1932), 117-30, and Frank L. Owsley, "Defeatism in the Confederacy," *North Carolina Historical Review,* III (1926), 446-56. Two informative articles in Texas were Edmund Thornton Miller, "The State Finances of Texas during the Civil War," *Quarterly of the Texas State Historical Association,* XXV (1910), I-23, and Charles W. Ramsdell, "The Texas State Military Board, 1862-1865," *Southwestern Historical Quarterly,* XXVII (1920), 163-75.

Other articles worthy of mention are James W. Silver, "Propaganda in the Confederacy," *Journal of Southern History,* II (1945) 467-563; Richard E. Yates, "Zebulon Vance as War Governor of North Carolina," *Journal of Southern History,* III (1937), 43-75; Gordon Wright, "Economic Conditions in the Confederacy as Seen by the French Consuls," *Journal of Southern History,* VI (1941), 195-214; Frank Lawrence Owsley, "Local Defense and the Overthrow of the Confederacy: a Study in State Rights," *Mississippi Valley Historical Review,* XI (1925), 100-99; and W. F. Robinson, Jr., "Prohibition in the Confederacy," *American Historical Review,* XXVII (1931), 50-58.

★

INDEX